Stripped of Shame

DOREEN STUMPF

Printed in the United States of America
First Printed June 2020
Cover Art by Victoria L. Hawkins
Publisher: Southern Willow Publishing, LLC
ISBN: 978-1-7347354-2-0

To Yeshua.

For Junior!
Until we meet again…

And for my husband, Robert, my son, Tommy, and
Dad & Mom.
I love you to eternity

Forward

One thing that is necessary in order for someone to be free in their lives is transparency. In other words, they must get real and be willing to confess their sins, faults, and failures first to God and then to one to another.

In *Stripped of Shame*, Doreen truly gets vulnerable. She lays her life story out on the table. Unlike so many so-called testimonies, Doreen's story holds not just the gory details, but a transparency that I truly believe will help others who have walked in her shoes. There are many things that Doreen has experienced that so many of us can relate to one way or another. So, as one reads and relates, the pump is primed for Jesus to let those healing waters flow over their soul.

We live in a lost and fallen world, saints. Many ask the question "Why did God let this happen to me?" The truth is, however, God is not the author of the pain, hurts, and wounds that so many of us have incurred throughout our lives. But He is the answer to them!

I believe that in *Stripped of Shame* you might find yourself. You may find, in Doreen's testimony, a little bit of your own testimony. Through her honest explanation of how she worked out her own salvation, you too can find a similar path that may very well lead to your healing, restoration, and redemption.

I encourage you to not just read this book like you would read any other book. Read *Stripped of Shame* through the lens of the Holy Spirit letting Him speak to your heart what your truth is. As you read, go to group with the Counselor, the Holy Spirit, and allow Him to show you that you have a Heavenly Father who is faithful to heal you and always willing to love you.

Victoriously,
Pastor Trey Dickerson
High Point Church
Macon, Georgia

I began working on *Stripped of Shame* in 2012 with hopes of telling my story as I felt God had instructed me to do. The thousands of hours that followed turned into eight years. It is now the year 2020.

This is my story.

Introduction

"I am the light of the world. Whoever
follows me will never walk in darkness, but
will have the light of life."
John 8:12

If you have ever felt like you were never allowed
to express exactly what you were thinking or feeling,
perhaps others prevented you, or maybe you had no
choice and had to restrain yourself,

YOU ARE NOT ALONE!

Why am I writing this book? I have been asked
that question time and time again. I have asked myself
the same question, too. After spending much time in
self-doubt and wallowing in a sea of fear of being
ridiculed, I knew there was a book in me. In addition
to that, I saw a deep need. When I looked into the
eyes of people, I saw the pain of not seeing their own

worth; the pain of not seeing that they are valuable and treasured. I saw them allowing their poor self-image and ungodly beliefs about themselves abort any hopes, plans, and dreams they had.

I lived that same way for so long, but after years of walking with Jesus, being transformed through His process of sanctification, and allowing Jesus to heal my heart, I knew I had to go forward with this book. My paralyzing forces were shame, fear, and guilt. I believed that I was somehow hopelessly flawed. Those convictions dominated my life. I was effectively disabled; socially, emotionally, and even physically. I simply could not function in society. At one point I was diagnosed with Bipolar Disorder and a personality disorder. I never felt safe or sure around anyone, including myself. I believed I could trust no one. I wore myself out trying to keep one step ahead of everything and everyone. Fear dominated me so much that I became an expert in self-protection. I was always fearful that someone would take from me. Life for me was a war zone, replete with unseen emotional landmines, snipers, and other dangers. I lived in a constant state of chaos, confusion, strife, and uncertainty. At one point it became so unbearable, I planned to take my own life. Instead, I experienced an event that instantly changed my plans and started a process of transformation, a transformation that would change me from the inside out.

It was God's mercy and grace that spared me all those years ago. Since then I have experienced great peace and release, as well as many challenges and difficulties. Yet through it all I found a power that is much greater than me that set me free. I finally have a peace that cannot be bought. It cannot be found in a bar, in a man, in a pill bottle, or in an alcohol bottle. It's a real peace in which I can now accept myself and those around me without fear of judgment and rejection.

My intention for writing this book is that through the example of my own experiences, I would give the reader a sense of hope. Despite the negative things you may have believed about yourself or the terrible things you might have done or even experienced, there is a way out. There is a freedom for which we all long. I lived with that terrible self-image, a yoke born of a life of sin and separation from God. As you read my heart which is poured out on these pages, you will learn some of the exquisitely painful episodes of my life: not for the purpose of dragging out dirty laundry, but to show you the wide-open door of recovery and freedom that there is in Christ. So, why did I choose to write this book? The answer is because the Lord told me to. He has reminded me to trust that this book is His plan. Despite my own fears, no plan of His will harm me.

I chose to use my real name to show how powerful the healing of Jesus has been in my life. I no longer have to hide or be ashamed of the things I have done or the things I participated in. There is true freedom in Christ. That being said, I have not used any real names of the people I have encountered for their own privacy. This story is my own personal story as I have lived it and witnessed it. It is solely based on my perspective and my perception.

My hope is that you may find what I have found, the way out of shame and bondage. All the risk and vulnerability in sharing my personal life journey will have been worth it. I believe that with Christ's help you will find the courage and confidence to give your inner self a voice and allow it to finally be heard. You may feel that your voice has been stolen or it may be that you just do not know how to express yourself. Whatever the reason for your pain and suffering, you can and will always have permission with the one person you might have overlooked: Jesus. I hope everyone who reads my book will, in one way or another, relate to something I have experienced and will get the courage to express their heart and inner voice. I believe all of us perceive painful life events differently, but we feel the same pain. That is what makes us the same. I believe offenses are offenses, disappointment is disappointment, and hurt is hurt. Anyone who has experienced these feelings knows that pain.

As rough as my own life has been, I am painfully aware that my experiences are not unique. Circumstances may be different, but the healing that we all need from Christ is a common ground for all of us. Some of you may relate to my story, while others may see it as completely foreign and strange. It is my hope, in any case, that the Holy Spirit will minister to you.

I know that He has something just for you. If you are not a Christian and you still choose to read my book, I ask you to keep an open mind. What worked for me may not work for you, but then again, it just might.

My prayer is that you will discover that you have an unforgettable story and that unforgettable story is you.

The Voice that Released Me to My Father

Suddenly I heard a voice calling to me.

"Hello! Hey, hey there! Open your eyes. Hey, can you hear me? Open your eyes. Unlatch the seatbelt. Can you hear me? Unlatch the seatbelt!"

What sounded like echoes in my head was an actual person telling me to find my seatbelt. Dazed and confused, with my vision blurred, I tried to see where the voice was coming from, but couldn't. I zoned in on just listening for the voice. I didn't understand exactly what was going on. Finally, with my vision clearing up, I saw someone. I turned my attention solely to that voice coming from a man who was on his knees looking at me through my passenger side window of my truck.

I thought it was weird and wondered what he was doing on his knees as he looked at me sitting inside my truck? I finally noticed that I was literally upside down in my truck and my truck was upside down, too. What the hell happened?

Returning my gaze back to the man on his knees, I strained to hear what he was trying to say to me, all while trying to make sense of what was going on. I kept my gaze on the man on his knees. I was staring at him because nothing was registering until I watched his lips closely and the expressive gestures of his hands. This man was urging me to unlatch the seat belt.

Finally, as if the sound burst out of thin air, I heard him say, "Find the seatbelt and free yourself so I can get you out of this truck!"

I looked to the left and saw asphalt. I reached out my window and touched the ground. Panic was beginning to set in. Frantically, I returned my gaze back to the man and started doing what he said. Panic had set in. My heart was racing and I was afraid. Shaking furiously, I did what this man instructed me to do.

"I think I can feel it. Oh, there it is. I'm trying. I can't," I whimpered.

Oddly enough in that frantic state, all that ran through my mind were all those movies I'd watched where the upside-down vehicle blows up.

"I can't do this, I cried. I can't get my hand down far enough into the seat to unlatch the seat belt and free myself," I cried. The seat had been crushed inward and getting my hand down far enough to unlatch the seat belt was hard.

"You have to try!" he yelled out again.

"Okay, I have my hand on it. I just can't. Oh, there it is. Okay, I got it." I pushed on the metal lock and heard a snap. As the seatbelt unlatched, I slid onto my head and shoulders.

"Okay, good job! Now come on. Hurry! I'll help you get out of the truck," he directed. When he reached to pull me from the overturned truck, I felt pain shoot through my body.

"What happened?" I asked him.

"You were hit," he said.

"What?!?"

"You were hit. Are you okay?" he asked.

"I don't know."

"Come on. Hold on to me," he directed.

I slowly walked arm in arm with this stranger who led me to the side of the road. I sat down and held my head in my hands. My head hurt so badly.

"What is your name?" he asked.

In my confusion, I honestly had to think about it. I had gone by so many different names in my life that I had to figure out which one applied here. This was a serious situation. I had to tell the truth about who I was and use my real name. After a few minutes, I slurred out, "Doreen, my name is Doreen."

That moment was so surreal. Slowly lifting my head out of my hands, I took a good look around. My eyes took in what used to be my life. Or was it that this was really what my life looked like?

"There's been an accident," said the man who had walked me to the curb. He pointed toward the scene and said, "There is your truck."

As I followed his finger, I saw my new pickup truck upside down. Everything that had been in the back of my truck was scattered all over the road.

He then said, "You are so lucky to be alive. Hang in there. The ambulance is on the way. Hang on just a little longer. Don't move, just sit there and be still."

The ambulance arrived and I was immediately surrounded by EMTs asking all sorts of questions. All I wanted was for them to leave me alone and just let me die.

Shocked, scared, and feeling faint, I sat with my life having just come to a complete standstill. The reality of it was slowly dawning on me. How would I be expected to go on after this horrible event? I wished I had died in the accident. Fear welled up in the center of my being and I remembered the need to keep conscious, if possible. I forced myself to repeat things that I was certain of like my name. Doreen Davenport, Doreen Davenport, Doreen Davenport. As I did so, I felt the old familiar emotional pain and disappointment associated with my name well up. Even the very sound of it made my skin crawl. I hated that name!

In my next breath, I changed from the repetition of my name to reciting the alphabet over and over. The last thing I wanted was to lose the ability to be in control of what was going on around me. I learned early in life that I had to protect myself and do whatever it took to survive.

"Hey there, young lady! We are going to put you on a stretcher and check you out, okay? There is a helicopter coming to trauma hawk you to Delray Medical Center where you will receive care. Just relax and we'll do all the work," a voice said.

The shock of the loss was starting to suffocate me and the ability to speak was becoming extremely difficult. As I lay there on the stretcher on the side of the main highway, my best friend, who I had been following in my truck, checked on me.

"What happened?" I asked.

"Girl, you are so lucky to be alive! That truck ran right into you!" she said.

Dazed and confused, I kept asking the same questions, "What? What truck?"

"That one right over there," she pointed. As I turned my head to look, I felt another sudden sharp pain.

"Here, help me up," I said. I wanted to see the truck that nearly took my life. It was a two-ton vehicle carrying forty-eight propane tanks that were now scattered across the highway.

The truck driver was being checked over by an EMT. He appeared to be okay. Suddenly I felt a little woozy. I noticed blood was dripping from my head onto my shirt.

"Just hang on a little bit longer, Doreen. The helicopter is almost here," the EMT said.

"Can someone call my parents?" I asked. Turning to my friend I found myself repeating the question. "Can someone call my parents!"

At the same time, I noticed that the man who had helped me out of my vehicle was no longer around. "Where is that guy who helped me?" I asked.

"What guy?" my friend asked.

"The guy who pulled me out of my truck. Where did he go?" I asked.

"I guess he's gone, but I think he left his number with a police officer on the scene," she said.

"I didn't even get to thank him. He helped me get out of the truck. I wish I could have thanked him. I can't even remember what he looked like," I said.

"Okay ma'am. Are you ready? We are going to tie you down and lift you into the helicopter. Ever fly in one these before?"

I quickly responded with a sharp "no!"

"Well, then this will be your first time. Don't be afraid, we'll be right here with you!" He shot me a comforting smile and began to go to work on my vitals.

Lying on that stretcher and watching everything that was happening to save my life was surreal. The fear that captivated me earlier was now completely consuming me from top to bottom. Everything had happened so fast. I was headed to Delray Medical Center by helicopter instead of by ambulance, so it must be serious. I listened while they radioed the hospital and gave them my information and the estimated time of our arrival. As he looked over to check on me, he asked again, "Are you okay? We're almost there, Doreen. Can you hear me?" The fear continued to crawl up my spine and into my heart like a big snake waiting to choke me out.

I was in and out of consciousness during the flight. Even though I had been told what had happened, I still could not grasp the whole situation. I was frightened from not knowing how serious my injuries really were, but I was most frightened by not knowing what to expect next.

I really do not remember most of the ride. I was fading in and out of consciousness and the pain in my body was getting worse. What I did remember was the fear and the thoughts of knowing I had just lost everything for which I had worked so hard. I remembered the look of satisfaction and pride on my dad's face earlier that week when he had seen how well I was finally doing in life. Today had started off being a good day for me, but now it all seemed to be melting away.

Somewhere within me I found myself crying out to God. *Oh God, please help.* This inward cry seemed to arise spontaneously, but was very unfamiliar. What I had always longed for was to leave this miserable planet. I hated it here. I wanted to die, yet something inside me obviously wanted to live.

"Okay, young lady, we are going to move you onto a table," a voice said. The nurses cut my clothes off, threw a blanket on me, and wheeled me down to X-ray. The next thing I remember is lying in a room while a doctor examined me. A police officer entered the door.

"Can I ask her a few questions, Doc?" he asked.

"Sure, come in. She's awake," the doctor told him.

The police officer began by expressing his surprise at my survival. "I just want to say that you are the luckiest woman in the world right now. You should not have survived that accident."

"Well thanks, I think. Can you tell me exactly what happened?" I asked.

"Well, young lady, you were hit by a two-ton truck carrying forty-eight tanks of propane. The truck was exiting off the I-95 ramp when the driver lost control and ran directly into you." The officer continued to stare at me in utter disbelief, punctuating his amazement with head shakes. "You are so lucky to be alive."

As I lay there trying to process the information the officer just told me, something else came to mind. I couldn't stop thinking about that voice that had come out of nowhere when I was being flown to the hospital. That voice had said I wanted to live and not die. It seemed so real, yet it was so foreign. Where did that voice come from? Whose voice was it? Was it mine? For so long all I wanted to do was die.

The officer interrupted my thoughts when he told me that he had contacted my father and he would be arriving at any moment. The officer continued to ask questions, but they all seemed to blur into incoherence. I slowly drifted off from the pain medication. The next thing I remember was rousing a little and feeling very groggy as I was being wheeled out to my father's car. I didn't have a personal doctor at the time, so the hospital released me to my father.

The Road to Recovery Begins

Even worse than the discomfort of the physical pain was the shock from knowing that my truck and all my supplies were splattered on the road. The next thing I remembered was sitting at the dining room table of my parents' house.

"Are you going to be okay?" my father asked.

I really didn't have a choice. My father had always told me I needed to be strong and I didn't want to disappoint him. I had to get it together.

"Yeah, I think so," was all I could muster.

"Okay, then," my dad said. "I'm going to take a run down to see your truck."

I responded with a weak, "Okay."

He and my son left. I had the house to myself. I was sitting there listening to the loud ringing in my ears when suddenly I experienced such an overwhelming emptiness. It seemed I could never escape my past. It was hard coming back to my parent's house, but there was nowhere else to go.

Once again I felt trapped. This house had memories. My folks moved our family to South Florida from New York a few months before my ninth birthday. My parents loved us as best they could and moved here to get away from the inner city and provide a better life for us all. But from the time I turned thirteen, this house was the one I longed to run away from.

Now as an adult, I understood the things I couldn't as a child, but those memories still hurt. I know that all of us have dysfunctions usually rooted in the ignorance or dysfunctions of those who preceded us. It was certainly true for me, just as it was true for my parents.

The atmosphere at home had its ups and downs, but for me, growing up there was horrific. My father was a former Marine sergeant and open displays of feelings were unacceptable. I was always told to be strong, which meant no crying. It was a family rule. My parents were always at each other one way or another. I experienced beatings with belt buckles and broomsticks. If I showed any emotion in front of my dad, I was in danger of being picked up by my arm and thrown into my room. My father had a problem with alcohol, but my mother's problem was emotional. One day I asked my mother where I came from and she told me I was found in the trash can. Whether she was just kidding around or not, I still felt unwanted. That comment put a permanent mark on my heart and for as long as I could remember, I felt like trash. I came to believe I could expect no better from anyone else.

The shame of it all was that everything had to be kept secret. I was not allowed to express emotions. If

Stripped of Shame

I expressed any kind of rebuttal, my face would be slapped or I'd be told to shut up. Worse still, sometimes I would be completely ignored. I learned that my opinions didn't matter. I was told what to wear, what to say, and basically how to be. I was shut down before I could grow. My little heart became hard and had no way to express itself. It wasn't permitted. My formative years taught me to believe that I was completely powerless. I hated it. I couldn't wait to grow up so I could run away and never come back. But no matter how far away I would run, I somehow always kept coming back.

I now had so much time on my hands after the accident that memories of my past danced across my mind like footage from an old movie projector. I sat hunched over the table in my parents' dining room in and out of those memories. If I had ever felt the depth of my powerlessness and loneliness, this was the time.

I felt dizzy as I drifted back and forth in between flashbacks. The pain went from intense pounding to mild throbs, just like the pain that screamed from my heart. I saw images of myself as a young girl in our home in Brooklyn. I remember being nervous and scared. I was only around four or five years old and I was standing in the dining room with my mother next to me. She was in a yelling match with my father. They were fighting again and I was so scared. Their fights were so common, but I never grew used to them. I was just a kid. I never knew what I was supposed to do. My heart ached. The fighting intensified and then my dad stood up. My heart was pounding in fear. I was all choked up and I felt powerless. I couldn't stop what happened next. I stood frozen, watching them.

Suddenly, I heard a dog barking and I snapped back into real time. I was back in the house with my heart still racing. Sadness overwhelmed me. The feelings and emotions I was having now matched the same feelings and emotions that little girl felt when she watched her father and mother argue in the dining room. The next memory I had took me back to that same house where I was sitting on my twin bed in my room wondering where my mother was. I heard ranting and raving before my bedroom door flew open. My mother appeared and she was very angry. I didn't know why. She came at me. I closed my eyes and took the beating from the belt buckle. I remember putting my little hands out to keep from getting hit in the face. She soon stormed out of my room and slammed the door. I couldn't say anything. I felt powerless and afraid. Where was my dad? Why didn't he stop this?

The present day pain in my head and body paralleled these old memories. I felt like I was caught in waves that washed in and out from the seashore. Time seemed to stand still, and at some point, I remembered my need for a shower to wash the blood out of my hair. I still needed to change out of my bloodstained clothes. My will to survive kicked into gear. I told myself to get up and take a shower.

As I tried to stand, the room spun around and I fell back into the chair. No matter how many times I tried, the result was the same. I don't know how long I sat there until finally, I got up and stumbled towards the bathroom. Hurting terribly, dazed and confused, my only goal was to wash the blood off my body and out of my hair. I wondered where my mom was because I could really use some help.

Crossing the threshold of the bathroom door, I suddenly remembered playing in the bathtub as a child. In my head I heard yelling and screaming. My parents were fighting again. Without really knowing what I was doing, I started saying curse words out loud. I repeated what they were saying over and over again. I felt strong and powerful. Those feelings were unfamiliar yet so exciting. I was four years old shouting out curse words. Suddenly, the bathroom door swung open and my mother entered. I froze in fear. I thought I would get in trouble for saying bad words, but she laughed at me instead. She then shut the door and never said a word to me about it. I was relieved that I didn't get a beating and it was in that moment that I realized that if I acted like her, I would be safe.

I shook those memories off and leaned against the bathroom wall for support. I reached out and grabbed the edge of the bathroom sink and looked up to see my reflection in the mirror. I needed to take a good look at myself. I checked out my head and my neck and touched my hair to see where the blood was coming from. I separated my hair with my fingers to see exactly where the gash was. That caused another flashback of my mother. I remembered her brushing my hair. She was very frustrated. She yanked on my hair and pulled my head around so hard that it hurt. She kept yelling at me to stay still. Once again solidifying those feelings of powerlessness.

Those feelings of powerlessness were still just as strong as I looked into the mirror as an adult. I took a long hard look at myself and gazed intently into my own eyes. It was as if I was searching for that little girl inside of me who was so scared, powerless, and helpless. That little girl was never permitted to speak. As I looked into the mirror all I saw was emptiness, sadness, and darkness.

I turned slowly away from the mirror and I prepared myself for the shower. I felt another sharp pain run through my body. I wished that I had been kept in the hospital, but the emergency room nurses said they couldn't admit me unless I had a doctor. What kind of hospital releases an injured person?

I held myself up with one arm and tried to bathe myself. I was in a whole lot of pain and I didn't have any idea what to do next. I was terribly confused. I had always made it through troubles by being strong and staying busy, but now I couldn't. As the water flowed from the showerhead onto my body, so did the tears from my eyes.

I couldn't help but think about the loss of my truck. It had been so much more than just a truck. I remembered the day I drove up to the Ford dealership to look at some trucks and get information on how to buy one. I was immediately approached by a cheery and determined salesman. I ended up with a new truck. I was so proud of myself because for the first time I hadn't needed my parents' help. I couldn't wait to go show them, especially my dad. I remember driving directly to their house hoping that he would be home.

I felt very much like a little girl who wanted to show her daddy her new toy. I slowly pulled into their driveway and turned off the engine. I opened the front door hoping to see my father at the dining room table reading the newspaper.

"Dad, you here? Dad, where you at?" I called.

"What? What is it?" he replied.

"Hey, you got a minute? Come outside I want to show you something," I said.

I waited until he came out the door. My heart filled with excitement. I was a proud girl and I wanted to show my dad that I was very capable of making it on my own.

"Oh! Whose is that?" he asked in surprise.

"That's mine dad. I just bought it," I replied.

I observed every facial expression and nuance of his body language. I finally saw what I had been looking for my whole life, the expression of surprise and, most importantly, the expression of a proud parent. I saw his approval and how proud he was of me. But for some reason, the excitement was soon replaced by a sadness that overwhelmed me. I wondered why it took the truck for him to show this type of pride over me. Was it really what I did that earned his love?

I watched him get in the truck and check out all the bells and whistles, all the while asking questions. I don't think I was really listening. I was just watching the expressions of his face. It was like I could see his thoughts. For the first time that I could remember, I saw that he was proud of me. It made me feel very important. Then he patted me on my shoulder and said, "Very good! I'm proud of you."

My heart leapt with joy. My dad said he was proud of me. I remembered not ever wanting that feeling to end.

I felt disoriented and I realized I was still in the shower. I must have been there for some time because the water was cold. I turned off the water

15

and dried myself off. I sat down on the cover of the toilet seat to think. I couldn't figure out what hurt more: the pain in my body, the loss of my business, my new truck, or the dreams they represented.

Truthfully, I cared less about what was going on with my body and the pain radiating through it than I did about the business and truck. I knew that I needed to get back what I had lost. The business was my pride and joy. It brought me validation and worth and caused my parents, especially my father, to be proud of me. For the first time in my life I felt like I had value. Now, all I could do was cry as memories of the past and thoughts of my now empty future kept flooding in and out of my mind. Everything was gone: my health, my job, my truck, my life, and with it, all the respect that I felt like I had finally earned from my father. I had spent my entire life trying so hard not to be a burden. I was constantly seeking both my parents' acceptance and approval. When I finally felt like I had it, it was gone.

In my injury-induced confusion, I dressed myself. My mind and body surprisingly did as I demanded. It was all just my human instinct to survive. I continued to have a parade of questions march through my mind, like a broken record going round and round. What in the world just happened to me? What's going on? Where was my boyfriend? The loneliness I felt was making it impossible for me to think straight. I sat there helpless and void of emotions. Suddenly I saw a beam of white light shining directly over my head. I heard a voice say, "You will be alright." With that, the voice and the light were gone.

Stripped of Shame

Almost immediately after that I heard my father and son return. They were calling for me. To their amazement, they found me in my old bedroom sitting up. They couldn't believe I survived the accident. They couldn't believe that I survived such a devastating wreck. As they both stood there staring at me in amazement, the question that increasingly demanded an answer was why had I survived? In the days that followed, I couldn't do a thing. I was immobile on my back and unable to care for myself. I couldn't even go to the bathroom or bathe without help. The pain in my body was so intense that even the medications weren't really helping.

The diagnoses kept coming like curses: a concussion, short term memory loss, major soft tissue damage, reflex sympathetic dystrophy in my left leg, temporomandibular joint disorder due to the trauma to the left side of my jaw, fibromyalgia throughout my entire body, whiplash, multiple sprains, and the discovery of degenerative disc disease in my lower back. I was told I wouldn't ever be able to walk normally again. I should prepare for a life permanently in and out of a wheelchair. At best, I would have to use crutches or a cane to walk. Running would be out of the question.

It's going to be a very long road to recovery. I fell into a deep depression. I wanted to get well immediately. I needed to get out. I needed my life back. In the weeks after the accident, reality sank in. I realized the severity of my losses: my business, the use of my upper body, and the use of my legs. The doctors experienced first-hand my angry outbursts and pulled my father aside and suggested I see a psychiatrist. I immediately felt a rush of rage go

through me and recalled a scene from the movie
<u>Tombstone</u> where Kurt Russell, as Wyatt Earp, roars
out in defiance, "You tell them I'm comin' and hell's
coming with me!" In addition to my physical
problems, were they now suggesting that I had lost
my mind?

I don't know exactly why I always believed that
psychiatry was for crazy people, so when I was told I
had to go, it reinforced and deepened my lifelong
sense of being crazy. That terrified me. What if I
really was crazy? As I expected, our first visit did not
go well. I didn't think that the psychiatrist really
wanted to help me. I thought he was just trying to
prove what people have always thought about me.
Then he started questioning me about my life history.
That went against everything I believed about not
being vulnerable and protecting myself. I wanted to
squeeze the life out of him! I finally told him he could
kiss my you-know-what! He looked over at my dad
who was shaking his head in a defeated kind of way
and told him how shocked he was that I had made it
this far in society due to my inability to relate to
human beings. I couldn't believe he said that right in
front of me! By the end of the first session, he
diagnosed me with a personality disorder and bipolar
disorder. He wrote me a prescription and told me to
schedule another appointment.

I had already been on a bitter spree of self-
hatred. I had major trust issues that prohibited me
from complying with the doctors, especially male
doctors. I felt trapped and helpless by my injuries.
The reality of regaining strength back in my body was
nowhere in sight since it would not move like it used
to. Since my body wasn't bouncing back, I couldn't

help but wonder how I would get back everything I lost. The doctors were sure that I would never again have the full use of my legs. They were unsure as to what I could expect of my body even if it did recover. Out of the midst of my fear, frustration, and anxieties, I shouted at the doctor that I would have the use of my legs. I was determined that I would not be disabled or lose my ability to walk.

The doctor looked at me and said, "Okay then. Let's get you started in therapy for your legs and back." That's the day I started down two roads towards healing my body: one good, the other bad. The physicians helped me along the way to physical recovery but at the same time fed and strengthened a growing opiate addiction. But even deeper, there were issues in my soul that also needed healing.

Realizing the Reality

In the weeks after the accident, reality sank in and I was able to piece together what had happened. My truck had been hit on the driver's side by a two-ton truck carrying forty-eight tanks of propane. It had lost its brakes and careened out of control coming down the I-95 exit ramp in Lake Worth, Florida. I never saw it coming. While I sat waiting on a traffic light to turn green, the truck came roaring down the ramp right at me. It hit me so hard that my truck spun around three times and flipped over. It slid down the road about three football field lengths. When the emergency crews showed up to flip my vehicle over, they found that the top of the truck was completely crushed, except where my head had been on the driver's side. It was a miracle I survived. I was knocked completely unconscious and don't remember a thing about the accident. The last thing I remembered was putting in my new CD and lighting up a cigarette.

Doreen Stumpf

The accident forced me to reevaluate my life. My injuries forced me into a whirl of new experiences: medical, mental, and emotional. I would never have otherwise considered the pains and memories I was being reintroduced to. In fact, I had been deliberately avoiding them. That was one of the reasons I was feeling so empty and lifeless inside. I was so clueless on what to do. My boyfriend of seven years was also at a loss. He did his best, but after the accident things were never the same with him. I was completely shut down. I was on so much pain medication and over time became dependent on them. The temporary relief they gave me and the euphoric sense I experienced was one of the few things that were enjoyable to me. I also noticed that for the first time in my life people seemed to want to help me. This attention was something I had always wanted and needed. I even had the twisted thought come to me that being disabled might have some benefits. All I could really concentrate on was how my life plans had disappeared and new ones had to emerge.

All my hopes, my dreams, and everything that I had were wrecked along with the truck. Plans to marry and have more children were obviously over. I died another death that day, apart from my long-held belief that I was already inwardly dead. The horrible reality was that all these physical and mental troubles were simply confirming my belief about myself: I really was hopelessly and uniquely flawed with no hope of ever getting better. My physical disabilities were declaring to me and everyone around me what I always dreaded: that I was truly disabled on the inside. I was crippled, broken and unfixable.

Stripped of Shame

I was thirty-two years old and faced with never again having the use of my body and legs. I would have to learn to live life with a disability and accept confinement to a wheelchair. Doctors told me that even with corrective surgery for the spinal stenosis there were no guarantees. They also told me that if I chose not to have surgery, I would need to live on medication for the rest of my life. These prognoses, however overwhelming, were not as frightening to me as being labeled permanently disabled. Not being able to take care of myself terrified me to my core.

With all hope gone, I felt like a human volcano filled with so much rage. The injuries from the accident were only part of the reason. I was also getting flashbacks. I was starting to relive vivid memories of traumatic and painful occurrences from throughout my entire life. The abuses, the violations, my failures as a daughter, as a wife, and as a mother all flooded my mind. All the pain was reaching a peak. I felt cheated and stolen from. I turned my anger and hatred toward God. I wondered why I was even born. Why did God do this to me?

With all the time I had on my hands, I saw my days turn into weeks and then months. I had time to reevaluate my life. My thoughts swung back to my childhood and came forward to the present. It was as if some sick musical score was being played out. It had finally reached the point where it all came together in a sort of exclamation point for my misery. The accident was the crisis where it all came crashing together.

My strength deteriorated. I could literally feel any confidence I had dissolving and doubt and hopelessness swam within me. Deep in the crevices of my being lived darkness, and beneath it, despair. I was barely hanging on. Memory after memory flooded my mind and all of them confirmed my belief that I had made a mess of my whole life. It was as if my soul decided to take a walk down memory lane to remind me of all that had happened in my life up to that very moment of time. The physical pain in my body, along with the emotional pains of disappointment and failure I had experienced throughout my life were dancing mawkishly together. The memories, so perfectly preserved inside of me, were now surfacing. Those memories, unforgotten and unforgiving, were paying me a hellish visit.

At first, I tried to suppress the thoughts. I had always been able to do that in the past, but this time they would not be suppressed. I tried to ignore them by telling myself things were not that bad. I told myself that I needed to be strong and move on, but this time I couldn't. There was absolutely nothing that I could do to block the thoughts. They kept flashing through me, pounding at me. Once again, I was powerless to defend, but this time I was my own attacker. I was at the mercy of my own emotions and memories. My heart that had been screaming for so long, but had never had the chance to speak, was forcing me to listen. Racing through my mind, bubbling up from deep within where they had been hidden, came all the hurtful words that had been spoken to me, about me, and over me.

I couldn't shake always thinking that I was in trouble. The ever-present feeling of believing I was never good enough suffocated me. I remembered the pain from my mother's rage and sorrow from the absence of my father's protection from her. I constantly lived in the conviction that I deserved the punishments. It seemed that I could never do anything right. My childhood taught me that I was helpless. I was not that valuable and somehow I proved it over and over no matter how hard I tried to be different. It was like living in a minefield. I never knew when I would step on one and be blown to smithereens.

My body would tremble when I would relive the fear I had my entire life. I desperately wanted freedom from this mental anguish, but felt just as I had as a child. The fear welled up in me and choked me with a soul level paralysis that mirrored my inability to physically move. My mind and emotions scrambled to find another avenue of escape. The only thing I could think of was run. But where could I go? I wondered why I had ever been born, if pain, disappointment, and rejection were all I could experience.

I couldn't seem to remember feeling appreciated or accepted by either of my parents. Why all these negative memories? They grieved me deeply, so much so that I could feel the weight in my chest. I felt so much disgust for myself. I believed that I was a complete failure, so what was my problem? Survival kicked in and I began to rationalize with myself. I needed to stop having a pity party and quit feeling sorry for myself. Indeed, another cardinal rule of my father's: no self-pity. I don't need to start that destructive practice with myself again. But no matter what I thought and how much I tried to rationalize, I couldn't stop my mind from racing. I could not stuff back the emotional pain that had suddenly surfaced.

Something had happened inside me. A switch was turned on and I didn't know how to turn it off.

With each wave of memories, I wanted to run, but I couldn't. I was a master at running away, a master of escape, but not now my past was in my face. I couldn't sneak out the window or just walk out the front door. I was powerless.

Anyone on the outside looking in during my childhood might have concluded that we were a normal family struggling to make a living. We were a middle-class family and my parents were determined to provide for their children. When they were home, my parents cooked, cleaned, and tried to have some semblance of outside relationships. However, their issues inevitably came out. It didn't matter where we were, at a restaurant or out shopping or even on vacation, when they erupted into one of their fights, it didn't matter who was around. It strained everyone who witnessed it, especially my brother and me. As children we were stuck in the middle of it all, with nowhere to run, nowhere to hide, and no one to protect us.

As we grew older, my brother became my safe place. He was five years older and I would run to him when I was afraid or when I heard the yelling and the screaming start to fill the house. He was my source of comfort and nurture. I was only sixteen years old when he passed away. Out of nowhere he got sick and six months later he was dead from leukemia. It was no exaggeration to say that he was my parent and a reliable source of companionship. He was the one who accepted me and loved me without making me feel bad.

Stripped of Shame

Grief set in after his passing and not only did I feel rejected by my parents, I now felt as though God had rejected me. After all, wasn't it God who took my brother? Was God punishing me somehow? Was it because I was a bad girl? As hurt as I was toward believing that God took my brother, another part of me felt as though I was justly getting what I deserved.

I was sixteen years old and filled with fear. I wondered how in the world I would survive without him. He was the buffer between me and my parents and their issues. His death left me having to face them one on one with no protection and nowhere to feel safe. With my mind scrambling, I had to learn a valuable lesson in survival, especially in this home. I would work real hard and prove that I was good enough for my parents and good enough for God. I would become a people pleaser. I would make sure everyone was happy so they would be happy with me.

Strangely enough, as one part of me wanted desperately to help and comply, another part of me was unhappy about the whole idea. It felt unjust to have to earn love. In my mind, the thought of people pleasing for love and acceptance made me feel less valuable and ashamed.

Within seconds, I was immediately overcome with rage and began an argument within myself. *Why did I have to work for the love I needed when others seemed to get it for free?* It was wrong and unfair. My feelings swung wildly back and forth and I found myself doing the very things I swore I wouldn't do. With my heart pounding in fury, I **vowed** that I wouldn't take it anymore. If people were going to make me work for love and acceptance, then I will **demand** compensation. I'd better get something out of it. I decided that day if God didn't accept me for who I was and was only out to punish me, then I really didn't need Him either. Was that who God was? Was he waiting in the wings to punish the minute I made a mistake? I felt this most of my life by my parents, but was God the same as they were? Was He not interested in my innermost thoughts, was He not interested in what I had to say? Was He overlooking me? I tried so hard to get everyone's attention. Even after three years of repeatedly running away and returning home, no one had a clue that I was in emotional distress. Being the family scapegoat, they called me troubled and crazy. The focus was always on what a bad child I was, not on the fact that my parents couldn't get along and I grew up in a war zone.

The confusion and pain spun me out and I needed to set some things straight between God and me. Since I was raised Catholic I was no stranger to church. Even as a child I attended Catholic school, so I knew I could go to the church to speak to God. As far as I knew, that was the only place to talk to God. At sixteen years of age and just a few weeks after my brother's death, I got into my car and drove to the nearest Catholic Church. I mustered up the courage to go in and tell God just how angry I was and how I felt about Him.

I walked through those heavy doors into that church. I marched my way directly to the front altar and I spit on it. I ripped the gold cross chain from my neck and threw it down next to the spit. I defiantly raised my middle finger towards the crucifix and told God that I didn't want anything to do with Him after taking my brother from me and the only love that I had ever known. I was so angry. If I have to work so hard for God to love me, then I don't want any part of Him, particularly if He was a God who takes those you love from you as a punishment.

I spun around on my heel and hurried out. I decided that from then on, I would follow my own rules and not be ruled by anyone else. The first thing on my list was to start collecting from everyone who had hurt me. I felt like I had just done something so very wrong, yet at the same time I felt that I had been forced into it, like everything else in my life. I was angry, lost, and I needed my brother. I opened the car door and started the engine. I knew something drastic just happened. Something seriously changed in me.

From that day on, I resolved to stop being the victim. I became the victimizer. I was on my own.

Good Intentions

I laid on my brother's bed in his old bedroom caught up in the web of my memories. I wondered if what I did in that church that day was in fact the real reason I was now laying here almost paralyzed. *Was God punishing me again?* I tried to shake these thoughts. I tried to snap myself out of the turmoil that was embedded inside of me, but I could not stop thinking that there might be some truth behind those thoughts.

I tried to move around in the bed, but it was difficult to move around without pain. I needed to get out of his room. It felt like the walls were closing in on me. It took so much effort, but I did eventually get out of his bed. I made my way through the dining room towards the kitchen. Something triggered another memory and I remembered when we moved to sunny South Florida. I was eight years old. I believe that my parents had the best intentions for my brother and me. They wanted to keep us safe from having to grow up in the inner city. I know how hard they tried, but somehow things never seemed to work out. I remembered how I felt back then. I was so excited because I thought the move would mean new beginnings and maybe my parents wouldn't fight anymore. I hoped we would be a happy family. Sadly, it didn't happen quite the way I thought.

I stood at the sink and filled a glass of water. Staring out the kitchen window at the in-ground pool in the backyard, I watched the water glisten as the sunshine danced on its surface. Despite all the material things in and on the property, the most important thing, a loving and peaceful atmosphere, was sorely missing.

I remembered how excited I had felt about moving to a new place. I had such hopeful expectations! I was registered in elementary school, which was only two blocks away from our new home. I remembered how enthusiastic I was and even looked forward to waking up each day. I was eager to see that my family and I would finally be happy. It was so different in Florida compared to New York. I saw kids outside playing in a neighborhood that seemed so peaceful and safe. There were houses without fences and a two lane street with barely any traffic. This was so unlike our old neighborhood. In the city, we weren't allowed outside unless my parents were home, which wasn't very often. When my brother and I were allowed outside, it was only to stay within the confines of our tiny fenced in front yard that was too small for two active little kids.

I quickly made friends and joined a softball team. Sports became my life, at least for the next few years. My brother made friends with a boy across the street.

Stripped of Shame

They seemed to have a lot in common, especially when it came to their cars. Things seemed to be heading in the right direction. I remembered celebrating my ninth birthday at our new home and life for that little nine year old girl was finally looking good. I stopped wishing to hurry and grow up to leave my family, especially when I saw how happy my parents looked. Our house was nice with a backyard graced with fruit trees. For the first time ever, I had my own room. My brother was thoroughly enjoying his newfound privacy as well. The move was off to a pleasant start.

Even now those memories bring a slight smile to my face as I recall admiring the backyard, but those pleasant thoughts are always followed by profound grief because of the brevity of that happiness. After about a year, I noticed my mother becoming depressed. It looked like she was getting homesick. She had been looking for work and wasn't having much luck. She had never learned how to drive, so she was stuck at home most of the time while my dad worked extra hard trying to keep everything together. Even though my brother and I were there with her, it didn't seem to be enough. I remembered how things really started to get tense and when the fighting started again, the tension was stronger than ever. I remembered how my mind started to scramble and how the fear of being in that home with them started to consume me again. My hiding spot was the bathroom. I would lock the door and cry out to God for help. I would sit in the bathroom hiding until the screaming stopped, then with much trepidation, I would open the bathroom door and peek out. Everyone was asleep or in their rooms, except Dad, who was sitting quietly in front of the television. Our eyes would connect. I saw his pain, which I internalized as my own, and then slowly I would turn and head to my room and quietly close the door. There isn't much I remember about those times other than deep darkness, sadness, and the many nights falling asleep with the lights on because of what I saw in the dark.

The only place where I found times of peace was over at my new friend's house. She lived across the street and just a few houses down from my brother's friend. Their family seemed happy. Their parents didn't fight like mine did, at least I never saw them fight. They were a large family with five girls. It felt very safe and comforting to be around a happy family. I often pretended they were my family, so I spent most of my time at their house. I did this from the ages of nine years old up until I turned eleven or twelve.

It took only five minutes to get from my friend's house to mine, but the closer I got to my home, the slower I walked. I always approached the door cautiously. It was a guessing game to see if my mother was happy or mad. I hated going home. By the time I turned twelve, things got progressively worse. It wasn't that my parents were struggling or the family pressure at home was more than a kid could bear, because by this time the chaos was a way of life; it was the fact that my dad never stopped it.

It wasn't long before my brother's friend started coming over at times when my brother and my parents weren't home. It started when I was ten years old. The first few times seemed innocent. He would hang out to wait for my brother, and in the meantime, he would play with me. He would tickle me and chase me through the house, play hide and seek outside in my backyard, and sometimes he just wanted to talk. It all seemed so innocent, but soon I found out the real reason he came over at specific times each day to ask about my brother and find out where my parents were.

It was supposed to be an innocent game of hide and seek in my backyard, but this time when he caught me, he started tickling me. I remember laughing and so was he. Then he tackled me to the ground and continued with the tickling, but this time it was more forceful and started to hurt. I told him to stop, but he didn't. He kept on and on and fear set in. I was so scared. I started yelling at him to get off me. The last thing I remembered was hearing the memory of my mother's voice telling me "Boys are not to touch you there." As hard as I tried, I could not stop him.

He told me I had better not tell. If I did, he would make sure that everyone knew I was lying. With what I believed about myself and how I was already nicknamed troubled, I knew I would not be seen as the innocent one. His laughing stopped and his gaze was dark. He was very serious. He made sure I was scared and then he left me and walked away. I lay in the pool of my own shame, feeling dirty. I needed to get a shower. As the water ran over my body, I cried and cried. My insides shut down and my mind was in chaos. *What was I to say? Who was I to tell?* My parents already were under so much stress. *What would I say to my brother? This was his best buddy. What would it do to him?* I wasn't sure what to do. My mind knew and my heart knew there was nothing I could do or say. I was silenced!

I changed so much after that, but no one noticed. I closed up and sank deep into a pit of confusion. I remembered hating that boy so much. Shame and guilt washed over me. The humiliation, especially when he continued to come over to hang out with my brother, intensified. He acted like nothing ever happened. How dare he! He caused me to hide when he came over. He had his freedom while I was trapped in my room.

I stared out the kitchen window of my parents' house. I needed to snap out of that memory. I was shocked to realize that now, even as an adult, I was still feeling the anger and injustice rising from my belly as if it only just happened. Here I was again, trapped in a home that I had always wanted to get away from. Much in the same way that boy forced me to lock myself up in my room disabled with shame and fear, it was like a never-ending curse. I had been made to feel like a prisoner in my own home. I had nowhere to run, nowhere to hide except deep inside myself. *Was it ever going to end?*

I reached down to refill my glass and remembered how I simply never felt safe. I remembered how I would wait and listen for the sound of his voice to fade. I waited impatiently for him to leave our home. When I was sure he was gone, I would come out and, to my horror, he would be standing in the dining room. He was like a wolf stalking his prey. It was like he knew to be quiet enough and wait for me to come out. When I did, he would stare at me. He scared me.

Stripped of Shame

There was a short time when he stopped trying to get me and came to our house to actually visit with my brother. He wouldn't even look at me during those times. I remembered starting to feel somewhat safe again. Fear didn't consume me as much and I thought maybe it was over. Maybe now I wouldn't have to worry about my parents finding out. I wouldn't add to their stress and contention with each other. I wouldn't be to blame.

But then when my guard was down, it started again as if he planned it or something. He always knew when to back off and when to start up again. It was as if he watched and knew when to make his move, especially when no one was around. The minute my dad or mom left the house and my brother wasn't home, he was suddenly there.

From the outside, it all seemed so innocent. He played with me and joked around with me. He topped off his deception with overdone politeness with my parents and calm coolness with my brother. What they didn't know was that it was all an act and he had fooled them completely. What supposedly was an innocent kids' game of hide and seek, or catch and tickle, turned into a vile game of defilement. His voice still echoed in my ear while I stood there sipping my water. I could still hear his menacing words telling me that I couldn't tell anyone, especially my parents and brother, or I would get in trouble. I believed him only because I believed that no one would listen and believe me.

So, I gave in, just like that four year old child in the bathtub who figured out if I behave like them, they will like me, and I'll be safe. By the time I turned twelve, I surrendered. Another boundary fell and my defenses failed. When he came by, I gave in. No fighting. I just gave him what he wanted so maybe I could be free from the fear that crippled me.

I hated it, but at the same time I started liking it. I was twelve going on twenty, but at least I was getting some much-needed attention. Nevertheless, the feeling of being so powerless consumed me and I still hated being a kid. I still wanted desperately to scream for my brother to come because he had always saved me before, but this time I knew I couldn't. Whatever wanted to keep me powerless was winning, the fear of judgment and rejection restrained my voice, and I couldn't express any emotion. I was silenced again.

When I turned thirteen, I started staying away from home. I made the last time the last time. I made sure our paths didn't cross again. If I wasn't in school or at the ball field, I was at my friend's house. I made as many friends as I could because I figured the more friends I had, the less I would have to be home. My parents thought I was happy and if I was out of their way, everyone was happy. It was a solution that seemed to work for me. The cuteness and innocence I showed on the surface belied the deep anger and bitterness I felt inside.

I reached down to refill my glass of water again from the tap and noticed my hand shaking. My whole body was trembling. I couldn't believe how just reliving those memories was affecting my emotions and my body. I took a deep breath and I told myself to stop. I needed to let it go and move on. I took a sip from the glass of water and made my way back to the bedroom.

Stripped of Shame

I crawled back into the bed. My body was aching more than ever. My memories were on full throttle and before I could get comfortable, another memory danced across my mind of the next time I was violated. This one hadn't come from outside of my family but from a trusted cousin.

Both boys had started out with the same behaviors. They both gave me special attention. They both would play with me. They both held me down, tickled me, and made me laugh. They both were especially kind to me, my parents, and brother. The only difference between the two was that my cousin took me places with him. He took me to the store to buy me candy or whatever else it was that I wanted. He would take me fishing with him and I remembered how cool I thought that was because I was feeling like a grown up.

I was around twelve when my cousin started spending the night at our house on the weekends. Those weekends turned into weekdays. This time it wasn't a game of hide and seek. The shame and guilt of it all once again drowned me and I felt dirtier than ever. I was so disgusted, confused, and terrified. Once again, I wasn't allowed to tell for fear of being blamed. I didn't know what would happen if I did, but thoughts of being punished crossed my mind. The only thing I knew to do would be to go to where I knew I would be safe, which was deep within my very soul. I turned inward. I knew that at some point I would need to stay away from this house and even from my family once and for all.

One early morning while my mother was still in bed and Dad had left for work, my cousin came into my room as he had done a hundred times before, but this time something was watching out for me. Suddenly, my mother burst through the bedroom door. What could have been another shaming moment was immediately stopped by her lunging at him. He jumped up in terror while my mother came at him like a wild lioness. With no time to put on his pants, he reached down and grabbed what he could. He then ran out the door. I was scared out of my mind. I sat frozen in complete terror, but I remembered how relieved I was. It was over for good.

Nevertheless, as soon as all the dust settled, the same feelings of shame, disgust, and trouble choked me. They squeezed the life and breath right out of me. I was so afraid of being blamed, but my mother didn't say anything to me or even ask me if I was okay. She just told me to wait until my dad got home, which scared me even more. I did what I had learned how to do from my experience with my brother's friend. Escape reality by hiding within myself. I shut down.

I remembered thinking there should be some kind of handbook for parents detailing warning signs of a perpetrator. I felt so alone after she closed the bedroom door behind her. I sat there all by myself all day waiting and wondering why she didn't come in to talk to me and ask me what happened. I was left swirling around in a sea of fear, worry and rejection. My thoughts were eating me up and my mind was scurrying to find a way to make sense and get out of all of it. I felt so empty and so worthless. I needed to be cleaned up. I needed to be held and loved, but who would love someone like me? I was trash, a reject, and a problem child. *Who would want me?*

Stripped of Shame

My dad got home from work and I overheard my mother telling him what happened. Then suddenly my dad was gone. I heard his screeching tires as he peeled out the driveway. It was hours later when he came back. I heard my parents talking through my door. Then there was yelling. I heard my dad yell out, "He wasn't there!" I walked over to my window and opened it so I could listen in on their conversation. My bedroom window was adjacent to the front porch, so it was easy to hear everything going on out front. My dad said he spoke to my aunt, but she didn't know anything. Then I heard him pop open a can of beer and there was silence. I waited a few more minutes and then finally decided if they were not going to come to me, I would go outside to talk to them.

As I slowly approached the front door, I heard my father say, "It was probably her fault." Those words were like flaming darts and I froze right where I stood. My mind went dark and I was overcome with confusion and hurt. Immediately I turned on my heel and headed straight for my room. Once I shut the door, the screams from my heart poured out from deep within my soul. I opened my mouth to scream and nothing came out. I literally did not have a voice.

I felt numb hearing the words of my father. *Did all boys blame girls for their misbehaving? Was this how life would be? Boys get to do whatever they want and blame the girl? Are all marriages this horrible with fighting all the time? Do all parents neglect their children? Was this what I was brought into this life to experience?* Oh, I wanted out and I wanted out bad! I hated being me. After the overload of reality and questions, I fell deep into a pit of isolation and depression. I was alone and empty. I didn't have a voice. I wasn't allowed to talk, and even if I was, no one would listen anyway. No one cared.

A New Name

The weeks after the wreck were filled with doctor's appointments and therapies that tried to launch me on the road to recovery. The doctors diligently worked on my body. They gave me all kinds of pain medication and muscle relaxants to help ease the discomfort. Unfortunately, what they could not help with was the constant pain that lived deep inside my heart that seemed to be taking advantage of my physical problems. The regular doctor visits would always trigger unpleasant emotions. I knew it was because my doctors were mainly men. Even though I knew they were doing their professional best to help me, their passive aggressive and domineering personalities provoked me. I really had issues with men, I just couldn't believe them. To me they were all liars. I especially had problems with them if I at all sensed that they were trying to control me.

My life had changed so much after the accident. I had no other choice but to get used to having nothing to do except be victim to the constant memories that were assaulting my mind.

I sat in my old room at my parent's house. I was doing everything the therapists instructed me to do to speed up the healing process so that I could get on with my life. This urgency I had to move on has always been something that lived in me. I remembered having this urgency when thinking about beginning junior high school. I felt like I was starting a whole new life and all those ugly memories of my earlier years in our new home would finally be buried.

I was twelve going on thirteen with expectations of a new life. I was truly seeking freedom from bondage. Fear, guilt, and shame had been my greatest enemies. I started seventh grade with hope and wonder. But little did I know that the experiences that I had already went through as a baby, toddler, and young child would eventually grow into fruit in my adolescence.

Getting up in the morning was like a fresh breeze. I skipped my way to the bus stop thinking of how much I was growing up. As soon as I got to my bus stop, other kids would start to show up. There were quite a few teens at my bus stop, including one boy who I spotted immediately. When he walked up, he nodded his head at me and politely said, "Hello!" Nervously, I responded "Hi." I couldn't believe a boy so cute would say "hi" to me. Maybe this was the beginning of what I was hoping and wishing for. For whatever reason, it made me feel good. For the rest of my day all I could think about was his platinum blonde hair and ocean blue eyes.

The following morning I gave extra attention to the clothes I picked out and made sure my hair was just right. Each morning I looked for him. He had an uncanny way of simply showing up right when the bus arrived. It was easy for him since his house was right across the road from the bus stop. He could have simply hung out on his porch and not missed the bus. Yet, he walked over and hung out with us and when he did, he was always smiling. It was something I couldn't overlook. One morning he walked up to me and showed me a rolled up cigarette and asked me if I wanted to smoke it with him. It was pot and I didn't know anything about pot. I had never even heard of it before, but he told me it would make me happy and laugh. He said it looked like I needed it. He lit it up and started smoking.

At first, I watched him closely. He passed me the joint. In that split second, I had a choice to make. Which did I want more: a friendship with this boy with the beautiful smile or an education? I went with the friendship with the boy with the ocean blue eyes. I grabbed the joint and took a few tokes. Nothing happened at first. The only happiness I felt was that this boy chose me to hang with.

He did tell me it might take a few days of smoking pot before I really got the high and he was right. We smoked pot almost every morning. We also smoked cigarettes. I was on my way to what I thought growing up looked like. Little did I know, I was still a frightened little girl inside trying to find her worth. I become very comfortable with my new-found pot-smoking friend. He was easy to talk to.

I tried to make friends with some of the girls at our bus stop, but it seemed like they weren't interested in being friends with me. I remembered how I didn't really have girl-friends. I always felt so different from the girls. Finally I just gave up trying. I seemed to get along better with boys anyway. I found it amusing because I vowed to hate boys and wanted nothing to do with them. And here my new best friend was a boy. We hung out all the time and I was okay with that. Who needed those girls anyway?

The pot smoking started to do more than make me laugh and feel cool and grown up. I started being late for classes and even got the courage to skip school a few times. It was just to hang out with him. It felt nice to have someone who wanted to hang with me and not take something from me. I was so desperate to be accepted and when he did accept me without wanting anything in return, I was in. Being stoned gave me a sense of freedom and I really liked the carefree lifestyle. All the shame, guilt, and self-hatred that I carted around weren't as strong as it had been. Most importantly, when I was high, I didn't have to deal with the screams of my heart that would rise up from inside me.

When I wasn't high, I could hear that voice screaming for someone to notice me and it would drive me mad but being high helped me to forget. Finally, I just stopped thinking about school or about my home. I simply stopped caring about everything. There were only two things in my life at that time that I knew would not betray me or hurt me because they both accepted me: getting high and being with my buddy. I didn't feel judged, pressured, nor did I feel condemned. I finally felt like I was normal and had found the peace I had been looking for.

One day I got to meet some of his friends. His sister dated one of the guys he got pot from. Those guys were older, ninth and tenth graders, who lived in the neighborhood. I thought they were cool at first, but I kept my distance. They reminded me of my brother's friend and my cousin. They were rowdy, loud, and rebellious. They cursed a lot and they teased my friend and me for being together, insinuating that we were having sex. It was very shaming and I remembered being very embarrassed. I didn't really like them, but something inside me felt like I could handle them.

By eighth grade, a new girl showed up at our bus stop. She lived in the neighborhood just a few blocks away. I just knew that we would hit it off. She was quiet and didn't look like she felt comfortable with the other girls either. It wasn't too long until she was a part of the smoke outs my buddy and I enjoyed every morning. The three of us quickly became a trio. We started hanging out after school at her house nearly every day and got to know each other well. At first it was all about getting high. We satisfied our munchies by eating anything we could get our hands on or we would go swimming. Then one day I met her older sister and she captivated me. She was beautiful like Marilyn Monroe. She had such a pretty, bright smile, golden blonde hair, and a slender body. She was exactly what I wasn't and there was something about all that that I thought I needed to be. First, she was a grown up and a very pretty one, too. She was always so nice and always shared her pot with us. To make things even better, she would buy us beer. I was only thirteen, but I always felt so grown up around her and loved it. She was exactly what I had been waiting for, someone to show me how to be a girl. I wanted to be like her so badly, I was sure of it. She was very girly and I wasn't. I had always been classified as a tomboy and I hated that. I was born a girl, but had never really been shown how to be one, maybe in dress-up but not in attitude and personality. She was so graceful and kind. I had grown up around depression and anger, so I had thrown away any dream of being a girly girl. Being soft and kind wasn't safe where I came from. I had always been told that it was more important to be tough and take no bull. That became my way of thinking and eventually my way of life, but all the while I wished I didn't have to be.

Meeting my new friend's sister was exactly what I was looking for without even knowing it. In a split second I knew who and what I wanted to be the moment I saw her. I wanted to be like her. I paid close attention, watching how she held herself, how she was not ashamed to be a girl, how she made it look desirable and even fun. I watched how she acted, especially when she flirted with the neighborhood boys, even the older ones. The ones over eighteen would also come over. The most amazing thing I noticed from watching her was how she was in control. She was the one handling those guys instead of them handling her.

I was fascinated as I watched her interact with her guy friends. I felt a sense of the old shame and fear rise up from within and I desperately wanted to get out of there, but my curiosity kept me hanging on their every move. The more I hung out and watched, the more the fear evaporated and the shame was losing its grip on me. It felt like I was gaining strength from the inside out. I was so desperate to learn, so desperate to be like her, and so desperate to be in control. I didn't want to feel fear anymore, so the more I hung out with my friend and her sister, the more I felt like I belonged somewhere. I felt good. A new feeling of being in control of my life had been born and was being cultivated in this new happy environment. It felt like I was finally starting that new life I had been waiting for. I needed a new name. I would ditch the name I was born with and I would become Dede. Dede would be powerful and fearless. She would be the master of her own destiny. Most importantly, she would make certain that no one, especially guys, would ever make her feel like trash again.

It Wasn't What it Seemed

After weeks of staying at my parent's house recovering, I was finally at a place where I could return to my own apartment. I was still seeing doctors, which had become my regular routine, particularly since this whole thing had escalated into a lawsuit. Instead of getting up for work every day and being a parent to my son, I now spent my days embroiled in legal issues.

Things also became very strained with my boyfriend of seven years. I'm not sure if he knew how to deal with all of this, although he tried his best. I was at my worst and not just physically. We split up for a while and that time of loneliness triggered even more memories of my past. At the age of thirty-two, in my apartment, I sat and reminisced about the years when I had become Dede. I remembered how exciting it felt to develop this new persona and have the hope of being in control of my own life. Dede was a new person, birthed from deep inside me, and fueled by the pain that I had hidden for so long. Dede was my way out. Unlike Doreen, Dede would evolve and become powerful. This new girl I planned on becoming needed to be taught before she could really be all that I needed her to be. She waited in the wings, biding her time.

Playing two roles wasn't that difficult. Since I, now going by the name Dede, was still in my adolescence, my life as a teenager was a routine. I still acted like the daughter of my parents. I came home at night and did my homework and chores, but the moment I left the house, I turned into a whole other person. I still hung out with my bus stop buddies, but most importantly I hung out at my friend's house and was secretly being mentored by her sister.

One afternoon as my friend and I were hanging out watching television, there was a knock at the door. It was a couple of guys who were friends of my friend's sister. We will call them Three and Four. They were cousins. Three was the younger one, but a few years my senior. Four was much older, in his early twenties. My friend's sister came out of her room to answer the door. She looked beautiful. Her hair was perfectly done, she was dressed nice, and her makeup was perfect. When she answered the door and these two guys walked in, everyone was smiling like they were so happy to see each other. I remembered perking right up and watching. She introduced me to them and we said hi. They walked through the living room into the kitchen. As they did, Three turned his head back and gave me a second look. The moment he did that, I felt a rush go through me.

This guy was so cute and had a great smile. They were in the kitchen for a few minutes laughing and talking when out of nowhere, Three walked back into the living room and handed me a joint. I lit it soon after he walked back into the kitchen.

From that day forward, I couldn't stop thinking about him. Since Three lived right across the street from my new hang-out, I got to see him nearly every day. My friend's parents worked all day and they got home late at night. That gave us free rein after school of the entire house and swimming pool. It became Dede's regular routine to head directly over to her friend's house after school. Three almost always showed up and I looked forward to seeing him.

When he showed up, he always had pot and beer. Hanging out and being able to party like that was so awesome, especially for a teenager desperate to grow up and be on her own. One afternoon we were all partying together out by the pool, we were having so much fun listening to music and swimming when we noticed we were out of beer. Three asked me to ride with him to the store to pick up another twelve-pack. I thought my heart would explode because he chose me to ride with him. I had a great time going to the store with him. I'll never forget that day driving around in his sports car. It had tinted windows and great speakers. On our way to the store, we jammed to rock and roll, all the while smoking a joint. I felt so special.

When we got back to the house, he reached over and kissed me. I was so surprised. I liked him, but I wasn't sure if he liked me at all. When we finished kissing, we got out of the car, grabbed the beer, and walked towards the front door. He leaned over and kissed me again. I was caught off guard and confused. I was very naïve about these kinds of things and didn't realize that I was walking into the same trap as I had with my molesters.

Nothing was said and nothing more happened that night. We all went right back to partying and hanging out. When he got ready to leave, he hesitated. I stared at him, looking for some kind of sign. He looked back at me and winked. It was our own little secret.

Each time I saw him after that, he was usually with his cousin. We usually did the same things: hang out by the pool, drink, smoke pot and cigarettes, and listen to music. I got very comfortable hanging with these guys. There was flirting, but nothing more. Then one day Three and Four invited me to go for a ride with them. I thought nothing of it. We grabbed a few beers for the ride and drove by the beach through town. When we finally headed back towards the house, I was feeling free. As we got closer to the neighborhood, they didn't drive back to my friend's house. Instead they pulled into the trailer park where Four lived. They drove to the back of the park where the laundromat was and parked. They lit up another joint but by this time I was out of sorts and more than ready to get back. They ignored me and kept smoking. Before I knew it, Three got in the back seat and started kissing me. Then Four got in on the other side. I was frozen in fear. Things became such a blur and before I knew it, I was being dropped off at my parents' house. They pulled up to the side of the mailbox and said, "See you later." I was numb as I stumbled my way to the door.

I went immediately to my bedroom and sat on the bed. Shame washed over me like a tidal wave. I was smothered in humiliation and guilt. *I asked for this, didn't I?* I felt like such a fool. *How did I not see it?* I'd been taken advantage of again and this time I'd put myself in the situation. The memory of that day never faded. I was covered from head to toe with so much shame, guilt, and more self-hatred all over again.

I wanted to tell my parents that I needed help, but I couldn't talk. I literally couldn't talk. It felt like I had a sock stuck in my throat. I was stuck with my own self condemnation, severely beating myself up and back to feeling like garbage. I had sworn that no one would ever make me feel like this again, but these guys did.

Not only was the person I was trying not to be covered in shame, but now so was the new person I was trying to be. I had made a solemn vow that this would never happen to me again, and it happened anyway. I was so embarrassed. I couldn't take the skin-crawling shame. I couldn't take the horrible thoughts running through my mind. I went into survival mode and immediately got into the shower. I figured if I scrubbed myself clean, I could start over. I would wash away the blood, the disgust, and shame. I felt if I could only get clean enough, all the dirty feelings would go right down the drain and I would be fine. I felt like I deserved this. This was a normal thing for bad girls like me.

I argued with myself that this wasn't any different from what had happened when I was younger. I thought of the times behind the tree in my backyard. Over and over I told myself I was fine. It was my fault anyway. It wasn't so bad. I deserved this. I was a bad girl and I was trash. I had to be strong and forget it.

No one noticed that I was in torment. No one knew. I relived those mortifying memories of that day over and over and over until finally I was thoroughly convinced that I could expect no better.

My home life was stressful. The constant bickering suffocated me. I desperately wanted to get away, so when I got up the courage to run away from home, I did. I was almost fourteen years old. I was found within a week and returned home. I don't remember anyone asking me why I wanted to run away or leave home so badly. I was treated as though I was a problem child with a mental illness. I wasn't asked what was going on inside of me that made me feel like I couldn't be a part of the family anymore. I do remember the looks on my parent's faces. That look that said we are doing everything we can but she was just so out of control. That look mainly came from my mother, but the look of disappointment came from my dad. I was sent to my room and eventually everything was swept under the rug and ignored. I dealt with my demons while overhearing my mother and father talking about me like I was the source of most of their problems. The worst was when I overheard my mother on the phone talking about her problem child. My parents were convinced that I was bipolar and crazy. I felt like such an outsider. Why couldn't they see I needed help?

Fortunately, summer break soon arrived and school was out. Junior high was over and I had another chance at a fresh start. I was going to be fifteen in just a few weeks and I couldn't wait. My plan was going to stay home more and be a good girl. I planned on not spending as much time with my bus stop buddies, nor would I go over to my friend's house to visit with her. I didn't have the guts to confront anyone about what happened between me, Three, and Four. I was so scared. Fear controlled me and I didn't speak. I stayed to myself and exchanged the fun I used to have for food, sleeping, and watching lots of television.

I gained lots of weight over the summer. I was terrified of going back to school and into ninth grade. I would run right back into all those people I was running from. Fortunately for me, the school I was supposed to go to for ninth grade was overcrowded. The letter I received in the mail informed me that my new school was across town. That was confirmation enough for me. When I started ninth grade, I met a new crowd similar to my last one. I had turned fifteen over the summer. Thinking I would stay on this new track, I dressed and prepared myself for high school.

One afternoon while sitting outside watching traffic, I happened to notice my friend, the one whose family I tried to be a part of when I was eight. My old friend was outside playing catch with her younger sister. I put some shoes on and headed over to her house. Passing by the house of my brother's friend, I shivered and recalled how he had taken advantage of me. Things had certainly changed from the first day we moved. I walked up on them and said hi. After some small talk, she told me they were getting her younger sister warmed up for softball. This piqued my interest. This friend was the kind of daughter my parents have complained that I wasn't. I started hanging out with her and eventually joined a softball team. Softball was fun and safe, so I dove deep into sports. I tried to fit in again somewhere.

I was pretty good at sports and started to find out a bit more about who I was. Sports helped distract me from the pain I carried. Even at such a young age, I was carrying so much shame. I still couldn't tell anyone. Who would believe me anyway? One night at the ballpark, I bumped into my old bus stop girlfriend. To my surprise, she too had joined a team and was playing that night. After our games, we met up. She said she had wondered why I hadn't been around. I made up some stuff and while we were talking, Three pulled up. He was jamming out in his sports car and I froze. I didn't know how to act, but he got out of his car and acted like nothing ever happened. He talked to me like we were old buddies. He was there to pick up my friend and take her home. After an awkward moment, they both left. I really liked him, but I couldn't forget what had happened. After I got home and took my shower, all I could think about was how it really wasn't the boys' fault. The fault really was mine. *If I hadn't put myself in that position, then they would not have done what they did.*

Those thoughts continued to convince me how wrong I was to accuse them of something that was really my fault. I finally gave in and I started hanging out with her and her beautiful sister again. However, I wouldn't stay at their house as long as I used to. We would talk a bit and I would leave and walk back home. I did this a few times until one day, Three and Four drove by in Three's car. They pulled up next to me and asked if I needed a ride. I quickly said no and they pulled away. All of us knew exactly what had happened, but no one said a word. Dede, who was supposed to be strong and fearless, had been knocked down and showed she had nothing. I'm sure this was why I felt even more confused than ever, but I kept on walking.

One of the times I was at her house, we planned to play catch. Three pulled up and wanted to talk to me. Curiously wanting, or maybe needing, to hear what he had to say, I listened. I don't recall all he said, I think I was just caught up in the moment of being face to face with him when once again, he caught me off guard and asked me to go out on a date with him. After the shock and confusion, I remembered feeling sort of happy that he asked me. I gave up and gave in.

I surrendered to the blame and acted as if nothing ever happened. I became just another girl he could have his way with, just as it had been with my brother's friend. Walking home that afternoon, I thought I would be excited, but the truth was that I lost all the excitement of trying to become the girly girl in control. I had lost all confidence in my efforts to transform Doreen to Dede. They both were gone.

The battle I had going on inside of me against being worthless and not being good enough was over. I gave up. Those painful, condemning screams of my violated heart still would not go away, so I had to drown them out with drugs or alcohol. Three could provide both, along with sex. I needed something to make me feel like I was okay. I was so desperate to shut that taunting voice up that I shut my feelings down and told myself to stop feeling. I accepted what I thought I was: someone to be used and thrown out. Everyone knew it. It was obvious. So that day, I decided to stop running from who I knew I was and fully embraced my new identity. I went out with him.

I dove deep into drugs and alcohol. I used them much in the same way that I was being used. At first,

I used them to relieve the terrorizing and agonizing thoughts I had. My heart still screamed for love, but what I had found instead were guys who acted like they loved me and really didn't. It was a false parody of love. The acceptance that I thought I was getting wasn't real. It was all fake. It only came from the drugs and from the men that were using the drugs when they were using me. Then it was gone again. I had long misinterpreted the smiles, the drugs, the sex, and the popularity for love, acceptance, and approval. I was so hungry for it that I fell for it hand over foot. I was continually seduced by counterfeit love. This counterfeit love not only stole from me, but also defiled me each time and left me feeling dirty. It had no real lasting life in it. The outcome of this kind of love was shame, a lot of guilt, and death to my soul. At this point I was pretty much used to it.

I started hanging out with Three and Four regularly. I started getting attached to Three and started thinking he really cared about me. One night Three and Four came by as usual to come pick me up. Four had brought some cocaine with him. This would be a new experience for me. I didn't know it then, but this was what was missing to help me develop into the person I thought I wanted to be. This drug became my best friend. It made me feel powerful and it promised all the things that I declared Dede would be. This was the ingredient that gave me a superpower and I wanted more. There was only one hiccup because as far as I knew, only Three and Four had access to it.

One Friday night, I went to my friend's house to spend the night. I got dressed up and ready to go out with Three. I waited and waited for him to come but he never came by. I was so disappointed. When it finally got so late, we decided to crash. My friend slept in her sister's room, so I could use her room. I don't know how long I had been sleeping when I suddenly thought I heard a tap on the window. I pulled back the curtain and it was Three. He motioned for me to let him in. I opened the bedroom door as quietly as I could. No one was around. My friend was sound asleep. I quietly crept through the kitchen and slid open the sliding glass door. He was drunk and started apologizing and said he hoped I wasn't still mad at him for what happened at the trailer park with his cousin. He started kissing me. One thing led to another and we walked to the bedroom. I was his once more. He suddenly changed. He quickly got out of the bed and put on his clothes. He turned to me, smiled, and said, "Thanks. See you later." He walked right out the bedroom door. At first, I was taken aback by that comment. Then the shame and emptiness hit. It wasn't any different than that afternoon at the trailer park. *Had I been raped again? I did let him in and didn't say no. So what just happened?*

Then came my awakening. I saw clearly that he didn't care about me. I finally figured it out. I felt so incredibly stupid. I was hurting inside and my heart was heavy with brokenness. My mind was racing in so many different directions. The rejection, the hurt, and the anger bubbled until I couldn't stand it anymore and I erupted. Enough was enough!

That night, I decided that the tables were going to turn. I made some serious promises to myself. The first one was that I would no longer be a victim. From that very moment, I vowed I would make these men pay. If they wanted drugs, I would be their dealer. If they wanted sex, it would be on my terms. No one would take advantage of me anymore. This was my new rule and my new plan. I was fed up with being an object to these men and I was fed up with feeling empty inside. I channeled that hurt into vengeance. Never again would I fall prey into the hands of these men and allow them to use me or abuse me. These guys were going to wish that I chose them and that they had my favor. I started visualizing myself being the go-to girl. I would have what they wanted or desperately needed, be it drugs, money, a loan, or sex. I would be the one they came to. They would be the victims now and I would be the one who would decide what I would take from them, just as they did to me. I would be the one tapping on the window to come over for a quickie. I would be the one leaving them behind. I wanted to make them feel as cheap as they had made me feel. The tables were going to turn for sure. The brokenness ran deep within me, the memories of behind the tree, memories of my cousin and how I had never been protected, flooded my mind over and over and over again. These were the coals that kept the fire burning within me for justice. These embers would grow into a blazing fire that would make them all pay. Meanwhile, the venom of bitterness stayed in the cauldron simmering.

A Devastating Loss

When I went back to my boyfriend's apartment after the accident, my son decided to stay with my parents. I still wasn't entirely able to care for myself. The medications were having their promised effect and I started to consume more and more of them. My ex-boyfriend eventually left me weeks after my return home. My spirit felt abandoned, dry, empty, and alone with nothing but time and these haunting memories that kept coming. To help ease the inner turmoil, I decided to keep a journal and write down everything that came to mind. Every time something surfaced, I wrote it down.

Journaling helped me to discover each time I had a pain in my body, that pain somehow triggered a corresponding emotional memory that I had had sometime before in my life. Similar to how a certain odor or sound will trigger a memory, my current physical ailments triggered older feelings that had memories attached to them. In a way, the truck collision had caused a connection between me and my painful memories. Emotions that may have been quieted temporarily were still alive and unresolved. Whenever pain shot through my body, my mind associated it with a very similar past pain that was still very much alive deep within my soul. It was as if my body and soul were speaking on behalf of my broken heart. Even though I was much older now and had long forgotten these things from my childhood, my heart had not.

I remembered back to the time when I started high school, so much had already happened to me. In that phase of my life I learned to perfect my partying. I started to go out with friends more frequently and saw how hanging out on the streets was helping to shape and mold who I would become. I was getting older and the people who were training me were my new friends. I met guys who sold pot. I skipped school a lot and drank even more. I was learning what really goes on behind closed doors. Slowly I started to transform into Dede. I was learning the ropes and biding my time.

The year I started eleventh grade, I was in and out of the house. I had tried to be a good girl and stay at home, support my parents, and be around when they needed me. It was the summer after eleventh grade that devastated me in the most unexpected way. My brother died. He was only twenty-one. A part of me died inside. My family had already been struggling for so long. The pressures of life caused so much chaos in our home between alcoholism and depression. I certainly wasn't any help either as my rebellious behavior worsened. When my brother became sick, life at my parents' house was unbearable.

Stripped of Shame

The leukemia took only six months from the time he got sick until he passed.

I was already in bed that night when the phone rang. My brother was gone. The screams that pierced our house came from the very depths of my mother's soul. The deep darkness that covered our house consumed us all. I could not bear it either. I felt like my heart had been ripped out and I was suffocating from the loss of my only brother. I loved him with everything I had and I knew he had loved me. The very next day, after crying all night, I picked up and left the house with plans never to return. The pain of losing my brother radiated throughout my entire body.

I never fully grieved the loss of my brother. I had held the grief in, as I had done all the other pains suffered in my life. By the time of my accident, my parents were helping me as much they could. They tried to be there for me at every turn. I began to see just how much they loved me regardless, in the only way they knew how. For the first time in a very long time, I was so appreciative of them. I started to recognize their own personal struggles. But deep down inside of me there was still so much hurt and so much brokenness that I had not dealt with. I still held onto those feelings. I didn't know how to make it go away. I wanted to tell them all the things that had happened to me, but I was so afraid of their judgment and the blame. Fear still controlled me, just like when I was in my teens.

I sat in that apartment alone with my pain. I relived my brother's death over and over again. My parents were devastated and were barely hanging on. My mother was having the hardest time, but I wasn't too far behind her. My thoughts kept replaying every detail of his diagnosis. I remember the doctors said the diagnosis was severe. They gave him a maximum of six months to live. The doctors were doing all they could, but nothing seemed to be changing. I was called in as the last resort to do a blood transfusion. Nurses hooked me up to a machine that would draw blood from my arms, but I knew a drug addict like me would not be able to save the life of my only brother. My parents were so broken. They held on to whatever chance might help save their only son, but I knew the truth. My blood was not going to save anyone. I needed someone to step in and save me just as I was being called on to save my brother. We all needed a savior, but there was no one.

His illness and death confirmed my own, especially for Doreen, as there was no turning back. Doreen would never have a chance now. Whatever was left of her heart, any chance for her survival, was completely blown to pieces. My brother was the only person on the face of this earth that I truly connected with and now he was gone. My brother's death was the most devastating thing I had ever experienced. Having to witness my parents break like they did was more than I could bear.

I felt like I was born to watch the horror of the pain suffered by those closest to me. If ever anyone could literally have their life sucked out of them and still breathe, it was me. I watched my mother suffer her loss and my father struggle to remain strong and stable. It looked like my whole family was being targeted for destruction and there was nothing any person could do to help. With my heart dead and my mind gone, the pain and the pressure were so intense that there were no tears. I couldn't scream, I couldn't speak, and my throat closed tight as a drum. I screamed from deep within my soul, but no one could hear me. I hated God and I hated life. I felt like I had no other choice but to leave. I didn't know what else to do. Everyone and everything was falling apart. I had to get out of there. I did what I knew to do: run away.

I walked out the front door without even saying goodbye. I walked to the neighborhood convenience store I called a friend from high school. She knew the pain I was in and agreed to come pick me up from that store. From that day forward I moved in with her and her mother in a trailer park near my high school. I returned to school. My friend did her best to console me, but a few months after my brother's death, I dropped out of school. I would not graduate with my class. Instead I got a job at the nearest Burger King and ended up meeting a Spanish lady. She reminded me a lot of my mother. We hit it off and she asked me if I got high. Before the shift ended, she told me she would bring in a gram of coke for me to try. The next day, she did.

She asked what I thought of the product she gave me and I said it was good. One thing led to another and I found myself employed by her to move cocaine. I left their house that night with my first half ounce of cocaine to sell. I bagged it up and went out and got myself a beeper just as I had seen those who I knew sold pot do. From that moment on, I was in business.

I didn't start out thinking this was where I would end up. I had fourteen grams of cocaine to sell. I sold it easily. I quit my job at Burger King and got into full time drug dealing. It wasn't long after that that I was at a bar and bumped into an old friend. He was selling his dark brown sports car for two thousand dollars. After a few drinks, we ended up at his place. I turned him on to some cocaine and after a few hours of partying, I had the title in my name. I paid him one thousand dollars in cash and promised to pay the rest within a week. I had the same kind of car that Three had, but mine was better. I headed back to the old trailer park where I knew lots of people had a cocaine habit. I sold out of my stash and raked in the money. I knew these people would help grow my business. I had no remorse and my heart was cold.

Before I turned seventeen, I was making enough money to rent my own trailer from that same trailer park. It was a block away from the Laundromat where the tag team took place by Three and Four. Every time I thought about that day, the fire in me grew stronger and my hatred for men grew even more. I didn't have any furniture, just clothes and shoes that I had retrieved from my parents' house. It was amazing what I could get by just offering a few lines of cocaine to someone. People didn't hesitate to give me what I wanted, but the bigger picture was still yet to come. I was focused on making money and getting even with men and with life. I chose the highway to hell and I was doing ninety to nothing with blinders on trying to crash. I was trying to die. I didn't want to have to think about my life and deal with the failures and losses, especially the reality of the death of my brother. My focus was on staying in business and making as much money as possible.

My drive for vengeance was stronger than ever and Dede was becoming more confident. I was getting better at being a drug dealer and was dead serious about what I was doing. I pulled no punches. Finally, the day came when the same guys who once took me for rides and took advantage of me came knocking on my door. My plan had worked. I didn't go looking for them, they found me by word of mouth. The tables were finally turning. Their sweet and deceptive talk got them nowhere anymore. I was in charge and I made it very clear. It felt so good to be the one who had the drugs and money. When they came over to score, they were caught in my snare. My plan was perfect. I was very generous at first. When they were nice and high, I would pull back, just like they had done to me. When they ran out of money and were desperate for more cocaine, I relished at the spectacles they made of themselves as I watched these grown men begging.

To get more drugs, they were willing to do whatever I wanted. All their ego, pride, and power were gone. I was very satisfied and very disgusted at the same time. I couldn't believe that at one time this guy in front of me was all that I could think about. Now I couldn't believe how I had been so captivated by him. He was not worth my time or my drugs. My evil plan worked and I felt the power and intoxication from it. That gave me the incentive to move on to bigger and better things. I was done playing and getting even with the boys from the neighborhood. I needed bigger fish to fry. These trailer park boys and addicts were boring me. I needed to move on to men with some real substance, money, and power.

Inner Vows Come Calling

Somewhere between building a reputation as a drug dealer, I fell in love. I was almost nineteen years old now. For the next two years, I spent time experiencing pregnancy, becoming a wife, and childbirth. I got a real job and tried the married life and mother thing. I was caught up in bliss and didn't come down for those two years.

Every time I looked at my son, I saw the beauty of life. He was the only male figure I would ever give my heart completely to. I knew deep down that this would be a bond that no one could break. Sadly, although no other person could destroy this bond between me and my son, the inner demons stirred by hatred and vengefulness were stronger and became the thing that pulled me away. My bitterness held the greater power. It was the thing that blocked me from the charm and pure innocence that poured out of a child's heart towards me. I did not know this kind of innocence or this kind of gentle love. The pureness that poured out of this little child was so frightening and unfamiliar. It didn't take long for me to run. All my demons were still at work inside me. My unforgiving heart still had its mission, regardless of the cost. My sick determination to bring down and destroy men, especially those who thought they were bigger and better than me, was uncontrollable. Power was my god and I pursued it with no thought of its effects on anyone else.

There were a couple of years that I did try to make the marriage and family thing work. For that time, I laid aside the plans I had been working on. There were some huge problems though. The first one being that I didn't know anything about being a wife. My only example was my mother and since I had sworn that I would never be like her, copying her was out of the question. There was way too much conflict. The second problem was what I thought men should be like, learning from watching my father all these years. He worked hard, provided for our family, and kept to himself by merely tolerating my mother. He did show me love and kindness, but for some reason he didn't protect me from the rages of my mother. He didn't protect me from the outside world. When I wanted his attention, I had to do something to make him see me. Anytime I remembered overhearing him say that it was more than likely my fault when he found out about the cousin thing, my heart knew not to trust men, especially fathers.

I didn't know how to be a mother. I did try to remember the good times with my mother, but it would bring sadness because it made me miss how we used to be when I felt happy and good. My son was born in the summer I turned twenty. Shortly after that my husband and I moved into a bigger apartment. By the time my son was four months old, the fighting began. My husband was coming home drunk and he soon started to get violent. In self-defense, the old me resurrected. Fear, confusion, and anxiety drove me into survival mode once again. I was scratching for a way to get out. I moved in and out of my parents' house like I was staying at a Holiday Inn. My son was almost a year old when my husband and I started using cocaine together.

After two years of trying to hang onto my marriage, it finally dissolved. I was twenty-one with a toddler living at my parents' house. The dysfunctional abusive marriage was another confirmation that I would never have anything good in my life.

I left my son with my parents and went back to the bar. The bar always felt like home to me. I could be anybody I wanted to be there. I opened the door and got a whiff of the tainted bar smell and took a deep breath of the smoke-filled atmosphere. Dede was back.

I contacted my dealer and bought some drugs. I was ready to get back in business. I still wrestled with guilt. *What was so wrong with me that I couldn't make it? Why couldn't it have been different?* It seemed like the only thing I was good at was living like a lost child on the streets.

I had no recourse, but to use the pain as my fuel and move forward with my original plan.

I always found myself trying to figure out what went wrong. As far as I knew, my parents were completely unaware of what I was doing or had been involved in. No one said a word to me.

Doreen Stumpf

I visited my parents from time to time, but I was still caught up in my stuff. The only thing I knew to do was to keep working at building my empire. After reconnecting with my dealer, I started to make real money again and opportunities started to open for me. I couldn't allow my feelings to have any room in my life. If I did, they would have taken me down. I knew I was living two lives: one as a runaway mother and one as a drug dealer to the neighborhood. I didn't care anymore. In my opinion, Doreen was dead and Dede had once again emerged.

Business was off to a good start. I had been dealing for a while and making some new contacts. I met this Italian guy who took Dede up a notch. We started hanging out a lot and meeting at the same bar. What started out as a new drinking buddy ended up being my new drug buddy. One night he asked me to take a ride with him. We drove about twenty minutes and parked behind a townhome. He told me to wait and that he'd be back out in just a few minutes. When he came back out, he invited me inside. When I walked into the townhome, things felt very familiar to me. It was almost as if this environment had been created just for me. As we walked through the sliding glass doors entering into the kitchen area, the guy who lived there greeted me. He gave me a look-over and then told me to wait in the living room. He and my friend walked over toward the staircase and I watched as they made their way upstairs. I took a seat on the couch. I noticed this guy had good taste in furniture. His home was nicely furnished and everything seemed quite cozy and safe.

Suddenly I heard my friend call out my name. I headed toward the staircase and saw my friend waving his hand to come. I slowly walked up the stairs to the door where he was waiting. As I walked into the room, I couldn't believe my eyes! There were scales, baggies, and huge piles of powder cocaine. I couldn't believe what I was seeing. I'm sure my eyes were popping out. After the immediate surprise, I looked up and saw this guy staring back at me with this curious look on his face. He slowly lifted his arm and handed me a straw.

"Go ahead," he said. "Do some".

This was ride or die time. I knew this guy was testing me. I had learned enough to know that he was seeing if I was an undercover cop or something. If I didn't take the straw and do some cocaine in front of him, I would be killed. I slowly took the straw and did a line of cocaine.

Within two weeks of that night, I officially moved into his town home and spent the next six years of my life with him. His townhome was definitely a step up from the trailer park. I was the closest I could get to the main supplier of power in the county. I was in the fast lane and this time I was the one driving without brakes. There were no signs and no stop lights ahead. It was like life was something out of the movie *Scarface,* starring Al Pacino. I learned very quickly how to handle very large amounts of drugs and carry a weapon. This wasn't like the small stuff I was handling in the trailer park or bars. This was big time!

My new boyfriend had a great operation going. He had so many middle men set up in local bars moving the drugs. The DJ's, doormen, and the owners of these bars paid us well. We always had special treatment when we went to those places, including the strip clubs. These were the hot spots. The money was flowing in every direction and cocaine was the midnight hour delight. I had never been in a strip club before and was shocked when I went in for the first time. I didn't know that things like this were going on right in my hometown. I was ashamed when I watched them, but as I had always done when learning a new thing, I continued to watch. Although I had no plans to ever be in one again, it sure wasn't my last visit.

I followed my new boyfriend around with pride. I watched all the girls run to him when he walked in. They knew what he had and money was flying everywhere. The DJ at the bar closed his eyes, especially when his nose and pockets were full. The owners watched out for him, because they too had an itch for the candy. I was the queen and I knew that I was going home with him. The other girls could hang on him all they wanted because I was addicted to the newfound power I had been given. I wanted all the drugs and money that was attached to it. I was becoming a part of the massive amount of cocaine trafficking that was infiltrating the county. It was like I was dropped in the middle of a mob ring and had to stay on top of things. It was intense. If and when I went to sleep, it wasn't because I was tired; it was usually because my body couldn't take anymore and I would pass out.

As time passed, I earned the trust that was so highly valued in circles like these. I learned their code of honor. I earned the respect needed to be accepted among them and to be considered a member of the inner circle. I had so much cocaine at my disposal that I was high daily. The silent screams that used to control me seemed to be silenced for good. I had found my freedom. I was numb and having fun. I was enjoying the sense of power, the midnight hour lust-filled fantasies, and whatever else our sick minds came up with. I fed my greed and held nothing back. Cocaine was my best friend. It was my everything! Cocaine made me feel like I was on top of the world and completely immortal.

After about a year, I finally met the man who supplied my boyfriend. We went over to his house to have dinner because this guy wanted to meet me. Since I had been with my boyfriend for a while, it was necessary for him to introduce me. I had no idea what to expect, but I was forewarned to keep quiet and only answer when spoken to. I wasn't sure how to take that since I still had the man-hating bitch living inside of me. I politely agreed to go.

The supplier lived in a normal house in a regular neighborhood with no fancy cars or extravagant decorations. I was introduced, and in my best lady-like fashion, I smiled and kept quiet. I waited to be told when to sit and spoke only when spoken to. Immediately following the introductions, I was patted down and finally welcomed in. I didn't look around to check out the place. I just sat quietly while they continued to check me up and down out of the corners of their eyes.

Dinner was served and we all sat to eat. I was asked a series of questions about my background, my family, and so on. When we finished, we went back into the family room and had an after-dinner drink followed by a tray of cocaine. Right next to the pile of cocaine on the large tray was a gun. I immediately excused myself to the bathroom. As soon as I shut the door, I started to hyperventilate. I didn't know what the gun meant or if I was going to be the victim of a murder. I knew not to take too long. I had to get back out there before they got suspicious.

When I returned, I smiled and played it cool, as if I knew it was normal to have a gun lying on top of a tray of cocaine. Within moments, the supplier picked up a straw and handed it to me. I slowly grabbed it from his hand and lowered my head and took a snort out of the pile. I couldn't take my eyes off the gun. My boyfriend took the straw and did the next line followed by the supplier. When he was finished, the supplier picked up the gun and held it to my head. He asked me if I was afraid. He told me that if I were ever to snitch or work with an undercover, I would never see my family again.

The next thing I remember was standing at the front door as my boyfriend and I were heading out to leave. I don't know how much time passed from the time he held the gun to my head until the time we were standing at the door, but I did remember that I didn't want to turn and have my back facing him. From that moment on, I wouldn't turn my back on anyone ever.

After that night, the flow of cocaine was endless. My boyfriend was getting more and more paranoid. One night he told me we were having a meeting with all the middlemen who ran for us. He didn't tell me why we were having this meeting. I started feeling a little uncomfortable because we never had more than one or two people over to the townhome. He was so high and had been up for days. I didn't know what he was up to, but something didn't feel right.

Stripped of Shame

When the time came, everyone showed up and we were all hanging in the living room when I noticed a Latina girl standing amongst the men. I didn't remember ever meeting her. Finally, my boyfriend made his appearance. He slowly walked down the staircase. You could hear a pin drop as everyone quieted with anticipation. They wanted to know the reason for the meeting. He finally spoke and said he called everyone together to tell them that from that moment on everyone who was working for him would now report to Dede.

"She has the power and she is now running the business! If anyone has a problem with that they can leave!" He turned and headed right back upstairs. We all heard the bedroom door shut.

I was completely shocked. I was just as shocked as everyone else. Some shook their heads and walked out. I didn't know what to say, nor did I know what to do. I had just heard the news myself. It was a very serious move on his part and a very serious position on my part. I had watched many things go down these last couple of years. People died in this kind of business. I looked around at those left in the room. Suddenly, the Latina girl started complaining. She marched right up those stairs and started cussing out my boyfriend in Spanish. Then, in a firm voice, my boyfriend said, "If you don't like it, you can leave right now, but she is now in charge." After I heard him say that again, I seized the moment and blurted out, "Okay everyone. The party's over." I asked them to beep us later and we would clear things up. If anyone needed anything, it would still be business as usual. I opened the door and held it open for all to walk out.

As soon as the last person walked out, I had shut the door and headed right up those stairs. When I entered the room, he was busy with the piles of drugs. When I asked him what the deal was, he just smiled big and told me that I wouldn't be completely on my own. He explained he had too much to deal with and he wanted me to handle the smaller things so he could focus on the bigger things. He assured me that we were in this together and that I could do it. Then he said to me, "Baby, you got the power."

I felt something grip me inside. I knew it was always meant to be mine. I had come full circle and now had people working for me. I didn't have to be running ninety to nothing anymore. The people we had selling for us came to me and brought me the big money, as I once had done for the dealer I sold for. I was holding my own and figuring out exactly how I wanted to run things. The experience from my old neighborhood helped a little, but this was different. It wasn't easy figuring out who I could trust and who I couldn't, especially when no one seemed to be happy with the change in power. But once they figured out things weren't changing, it was full steam ahead. Selling, weighing out drugs, and bagging became my life. Eventually the Latina girl and I started hanging out and developed a friendship.

It was amazing how much the business grew over the couple of years. We were driving nice cars and carrying two beepers each. I draped myself in jewelry and nice clothes. I was living the drug dealer's dream. I had everything that I wanted. I was living in a townhome and my trailer park days were over.

Cocaine, money, bars, and power were mine, largely in part to the drug dealer's cardinal rule: never do your own products until you have sold what is needed. Always make your money and re-up. I followed this rule religiously. I developed some influence and my boyfriend became more and more trusting of me. I welcomed his approval of me, but at the same time I became weary. We had been together just over three years when it all started to change. My boyfriend became slack and started to consume more and more drugs. He broke the cardinal rule. We began arguing about his consumption. At one point, I considered that he might be jealous of how people noticed me before him, called me instead of him, and liked me better than him. Because of that, he began to act out by trying to sabotage me.

He started disappearing for longer periods of time and the rumors came rushing in. Days turned into nights and nights into days. What started out as a partnership turned into me running the business alone. I started doing more drugs to stay awake. I would be up for days at a time. I started slacking just as he had. I couldn't shake the lingering thought that he wanted me to fail and may have even initiated my demise. I refused to give in. I couldn't let him win. I had the power and I was not giving that up. My boyfriend had lost his power and influence and I saw the jealousy in his eyes. I watched how paranoia got the best of him. He started tearing apart remote controls and checked the televisions and my beepers. He started to suspect me of being undercover and began checking the car. He went through my purse and my things. He checked my cell phone and had me watched.

The paranoia got so out of control that I decided to stay with the Latina girl for a couple of days. I got a call from someone needing to pick up and wanted to know if my boyfriend and I were still in business. There was a new guy in town who had just moved in from Miami. He was Italian and had just bought a nightclub in town and was in the process of renovating it.

Loyalty and respect was big on the street, especially in this kind of business. The Latina and I headed out to our usual bar hoping to find out more. As we walked in, I happened to catch a glimpse of one of the guys that worked for me talking with some Italian. Things started not to feel right. I knew I needed to get back with my boyfriend. I had to tell him what was going on. We had to get things straight again or there would be trouble.

Putting all of our issues aside, I called my boyfriend. I left and we met up with him. We regrouped and put a plan in place. The Latina and I would be seen together as much as possible, giving off the impression that there were still issues with me and my boyfriend. If at all possible befriend the Italians who were now scoping out our territory. The plan worked and before we knew it, we were approached by a couple of the Italians. Their boss wanted to schedule a meeting in their new club after hours around three am. We agreed to meet with them. When the night ended, we headed back to the townhome and told my boyfriend all that went down. He left the room and called his guy. I wasn't a part of the conversation, but when he finished his call and returned to the room, we were told to go to the meeting. I was scared, but I couldn't show any fear.

The Latina girl and I prepared for the night. We stayed close beside each other and discussed possible scenarios. When 2:30 a.m. came around, we headed out. The streets were dark with barely any cars on the road. Wide-eyed and a bit frightened, I felt like Bonnie from Bonnie and Clyde as we slowly crept into the parking lot of the night club. We parked the car a good distance from the door and watched. After a few minutes and a few snorts, we exited the car and slowly walked up to the door.

The door slowly opened as we approached and we were politely escorted in. We were patted down and ordered to surrender our purses so they could search them. They offered us drinks and told us to wait. A few minutes later a sleek, smooth-walking man came through a door dressed in white. He sat down in the leather chair, crossed his legs, and smiled. I had seen those smiles too many times to not notice the look of hunger that radiated out of man.

After some introductions and small talk, he spoke frankly. He wanted all our business, our pagers, and our contacts. He would even purchase our product, but most of all he wanted our territory. He threw us a bag of cocaine and said our people wouldn't be disappointed. He was giving us a sample of what he would offer our customers. We didn't touch it. We told him we would get back in contact and got up to leave. We were escorted to the door. She and I walked as calmly as possible back to the car, the whole time feeling like a bullet was headed right for the back of our heads.

That night marked the beginning of a cold war on the streets. It was known within just a couple of weeks that the Italians had come up against the Venezuelans and there was a fight for territory. A lot of changes happened after that night and loyalties changed. No one was who they said they were anymore. People had been bought. My boyfriend's paranoia grew worse after that night. He was convinced that I was now playing on both sides of the fence. He took the business back, including my beepers and started running everything again. He said he did that only in order to protect me. The truth was he was paranoid. He ended up hiring a small time bodyguard to watch over me and take me whenever I wanted to go out. This guy was no more than a big babysitter.

My boyfriend and I had been together for a long time and we had promised each other that we would have each other's back. But when he stopped including me and staying out all night and didn't come home, my world started falling apart. I was so used to being with him all the time. It felt no different than when Three and Four dropped me off in front of my parents' house after having their way with me. I hated that feeling of being abandoned, so I started hunting him down. When I found him, he usually was at other women's houses. The rumors were true. I had to suck it up and decide what to do on my own. A few days went by and he called to say he was sorry. He wanted to take me out on a date and we would start over. He said he needed me. As I had done in the past, I gave in. I gave in to his begging and said I would go, not knowing that he had another motive. He said he would send his bodyguard to pick me up, treat me, and take me out. He promised to meet up with me later.

We didn't quite make it to the nightclub where we were supposed to meet up with my boyfriend. The bodyguard told me we were meeting my boyfriend at a customer's house who lived about twenty miles west of our usual bar. As we were headed out, he asked me to pull over so we could do a few lines of coke. As soon as I pulled off onto a dark dirt road, he pulled out a gun and pointed it at my head. I froze. My eyes were popping out of my head. This guy was hired to kill me. I started screaming. He suddenly put the gun down and said he couldn't do it. He just couldn't kill me.

Thankfully this guy was no cold-blooded killer. If he had been, I'd be dead. I was set up by my own boyfriend to take me out for good. The minute he put that gun down and started saying he couldn't kill me, I hit the gas pedal. I drove to the nearest gas station as fast as I could. We both got out of the car. My mind was scrambling. I don't know what I was thinking, but I made sure people saw us there together. I went to the ladies' room to catch my breath.

Once I came out, he was still sitting in the passenger seat. I got in and drove back into town to the nearest bar. When I got out, I threw him the keys and left. I was being watched over by something that night and was glad to be alive. My boyfriend wanted to get rid of me. I thought I could trust him, but he was just another man who took advantage of me. He actually wanted me dead. I beeped him from the bar and he called back within minutes. To test him, I told him what happened and all he said was, "Really?" The way he said it gave him away. He asked if I was all right and said he wanted to come get me. When I said no he started with the sweet talk. With a resounding no, I hung up the phone. I got a ride back to the townhome, raced in, grabbed my things, and left.

I'd get mine again. I was no stranger to waiting for an opportune time to move. Time was always on my side. This wasn't any different from my early days. I was used to waiting and one thing was certain, I always did what I set out to do.

My ego had grown enormously and my revengeful hurting heart needed its prey. Once again, I found myself broken, disappointed, and used by a man. The crushing disappointment that followed an initial rush of excitement and hope had become all too familiar. Just like that eight-year old who expected all to go well when she moved to Florida with her family, I found myself becoming the victim of predators who only wanted to take from me.

I moved out of the Latina's house and found a new roommate, a girl that I used to sell to. I had lost my cocaine contact, my boyfriend, and I wouldn't dare call his guy. Trying to re-up was impossible. After what all happened, I really had nowhere to go. I dared not trust the Italian. I was at a loss and desperation was creeping in. My addiction to the power, money, and the drug was strong. I needed to get high. I needed to get back in business.

One day my roommate desperately scanned the classifieds for a job as a waitress. She mentioned how a friend of hers worked in a strip bar and made hundreds of dollars a night. She was considering doing that, too. That didn't sound too great to me. I had only ever been in one to sell drugs with my ex-boyfriend. She asked me if I would go with her when she applied at some local clubs. I told her I would.

We drove around checking out clubs and ended up at one that looked pretty nice from the outside. She asked to speak to the owner. When he came out he looked us both over and invited us to his office. The interview questions were very simple. I caught him gazing intently at our bodies. Fixing his gaze on me, he started to ask me if I had ever danced before. Knowing what he was getting ready to ask, I quickly interrupted and firmly told him that I was only interested in a waitressing job. We were both hired on the spot. I was starting over once again. I liked the feeling of being in total control. I was back to rebuilding and had high hopes of getting myself back on top.

Within a week I bumped into a guy who had been a small time dealer in our town. I remembered him as one of my customers. I remembered thinking that he was just a dope head. He was always so low key and very quiet. However, my ears perked right up when I found out that the only reason he bought from me was to compare my product with what he was getting from his source. I needed a contact and he had one. One thing led to another and I was back in business.

Strangely enough, no matter how much I hated men, I knew I needed them to help me achieve what I wanted to do. I had set out so long ago to get even, to deal out to these men the same as what they had always dealt to me. I wanted them to feel just as much shame and guilt as I felt. I had been able to do that to some of them, but I still felt unfulfilled. My wounded heart was sick and merciless and craved satisfaction at any cost. Deep down inside I felt the tug of incompleteness. I still had one more important conquest before I would be satisfied. In my mind, it wasn't over until I said it was over, and I wanted to have everything.

Doreen Stumpf

Working as a waitress in a strip club gave me a home court advantage. Who else but me could go into the dressing rooms with an ounce of cocaine and sell all of it by mid morning? I was rolling big within days. The money was back in my hands and the straw back up my nose.

I had seriously believed that my ex-boyfriend was the one with the power, and to some degree he was, but not too many people liked him. My new contact was cool, quiet, and well-liked. Out of all the people that I met in this racket, he seemed responsible, but I still knew better to be naïve enough to put my trust in him.

Waitressing allowed me the access I needed to sell my drugs, but I started getting greedy. I didn't just want the money, but also power. What I considered real power was what I witnessed back when I was just a teenager watching my friend's sister handle those men from the neighborhood. It was the same power I saw each time I watched a girl dance in front of a man as she watched him empty out his wallet. I wanted that power. I saw how I could not only take the girls' money, but I could take the men's money, too. I wanted it all and I was going to have it all. I bought some boots and a new dancing costume. I told the owner I was ready to dance and CC was born.

High Times

My life was looking good. In just two short months, I was back on top. I could walk into the strip club and the DJ would announce me like a star. I was treated with respect and people were at my beck and call. These were high times for me. I wished my ex-boyfriend, Three, and all the boys who used me could see me living my high life. I wanted to rub it all in their faces, but I knew I had to watch my back. I knew better than to step over the line between my ex-boyfriend and the Venezuelans. I also knew better than to cross the Italians. I kept low-key at first and stayed within my boundaries. I needed to reestablish my reputation. I was soon known as "CC," which stood for cocaine.

The cocaine and I were one. It was my only friend and it didn't betray me. It gave me money, cars, and jewelry. It brought me the comfort I needed. It put me on top of the world. I was in charge when cocaine was on my side. It protected me and gave me everything I wanted when I wanted it. It didn't cheat on me or take advantage of me. It gave me the advantage I always wanted and I took all that I could get my hands on.

My reputation started to grow as it had before. I was getting calls all hours of the night and I knew I needed help. Since I was working in the strip clubs, I picked up some help who would do my running for me. This time they wouldn't be men. I was forming my own circle and they would be women. While I was in the midst of building my empire of power, I found out that my ex-boyfriend had slipped up again. This time it was worse than ever. He had been isolating himself and wasn't doing business. A former runner of ours came to buy from me and filled me in on the details. He told me the last time he saw my ex-boyfriend, he was acting paranoid and looked horrible. His circle of people had tried to stay with him, but they were getting spooked by his behavior and had to find contacts elsewhere. They all soon scattered and left him in the dust. I almost felt bad for him.

CC was ruthless and after all the crap this man put me through, I truthfully didn't care about him anymore. CC was who I was now and she was cold. She only cared about cash and always had a supply of cocaine. I reveled in my new identity and enjoyed my money, my drugs, and the power.

My revenge was taking on a completely new form and it really didn't require too much work. I was getting better at raping men of their dignity. I took their money and left them begging and wanting more. My evil heart had fully ripened, but its bitter root was consuming me. Pain and torment were now running my life. The problem with a broken heart is that it wants to break more hearts. I needed satisfaction, but it never seemed that enough was enough. I was never really satisfied. When it came to getting even with men, my heart was out for blood and it wouldn't stop until it drew more and more. I was always out for more.

My Firebird with a 402 engine and T-tops was running as smooth as I was. I had the keys to my own kingdom and no one was going to take advantage of me again. I moved out of my friend's house and moved into a villa. I went shopping every day for new jewelry. I was having fun. Those were certainly high times in more ways than one.

I started to notice a man coming into the club often. He liked to stop in to talk to a few dancers before disappearing. This man could not be inconspicuous even if he tried. He was a huge body-builder type. He was big, he was black, and he was good looking! One night our eyes met. I watched him slowly make his way over to the table where I said hello. He offered to buy me a drink. After some small talk, he said he knew who I was and what I was capable of. He wanted to know if I knew any girls who wanted to make some money on the side providing some "private" company. He said it could be lucrative and I knew exactly what he meant.

The idea of making more money without doing the work sounded good to me. I told him I would think about it and we would talk again, but in my mind I started a second business that night. My greed knew no bounds and I used women just as badly as I used men. I got so money hungry that everyone became objects to me. They were all commodities and

Doreen Stumpf

I was in the merchandising business with people as my products. I connected women with men who would pay for their attention. I had turned into a monster. Everyone needs money, everyone needs attention, and everyone likes to get high, and I was offering all three.

My abused and injured heart guided me. This was the ultimate outcome of my shame and guilt. In my opinion, these types of men who purchased sex deserved to be taken advantage of. They deserved to have everything taken from them. My youthful experiences taught me to believe that all men were selfish. I believed that all men lie, cheat, rape, and take what doesn't belong to them. They certainly did hurt and break me over and over again. My shattered heart needed revenge in order to compensate for all that had been taken from me. I hoped that once the drugs and the partying were all over, that same shame and guilt and loneliness would wash over them. I wanted them to feel like the filthy rodents I knew they were.

My new partner schooled me in the game of setting up dates and it was through this I met Mr. Palm Beach. The Palm Beach lifestyle was so different from what I had ever experienced. I started in the trailer park and I moved up and into Palm Beach! At first I was intimidated by the lifestyle and wealth in Palm Beach. These people owned yachts and drove expensive cars like Jaguars, Porsches, and BMWs. They owned homes right on the beach. Palm Beach was so beautiful, like something out of a magazine. It was upscale, classy and clean.

I met so many people right away. Girls were coming and going and so was the money. I was actually having fun allowing my inhibitions to run wild. I enjoyed dressing up, meeting new people, finding new upscale bars, and visiting the beach. The sunrise was always my favorite. Mr. Palm Beach showed me around and introduced me to so many people. My black book was growing and so was my purse. As our relationship grew stronger and trust was established, he asked me to move in. He had a spare room and living in his home seemed like a perfect business arrangement. He guaranteed a steady income for me and I guaranteed a steady stream of women for him and his friends.

I didn't have to show up at the strip club as much, since this second business started to provide the income I needed to support my lifestyle. When I did show up, it was mostly to keep the inventory of women fresh and well stocked for Mr. Palm Beach and his friends. I was completely immersed in my new identity. I enjoyed living a life of extravagance for around a year. I had access to great food, great clothes, a gorgeous home, an endless supply of cash, and drugs. I finally felt satisfied that I had reached what I had set out to do.

The men I met presented themselves as businessmen. They were clean cut, wore nice clothes and shoes, and had a wallet full of money and credit cards. They drove nice cars. They were white collar business men who spoke clear concise English. This crowd made their wealth from lucrative business ventures, unlike the hustle I was dishing out. These guys were educated and used their brains to make their money. They cut loose, but they knew when to stop and get back to their ventures. There was something so intriguing to their secrecy and how they lived their lives. I wanted to learn more. The feeling of inferiority soon left me, and I believed I could fit in just as well as anyone of them. As soon as I set my mind to do that, my connections and business grew.

Mr. Palm Beach purchased a building in Miami and asked me if I would consider moving there to help him run it. Miami Beach is the home of the rich and famous. I had thought Palm Beach was something, but Miami Beach was where it was all happening. Now I would be able to live there. I couldn't wait to move. Miami Beach was Florida's most prestigious vacation spot. Many Hollywood stars, local actors and actresses, college students, and tourists from all over the world visited Miami. The beautiful white sandy beaches and the night life was an attraction. It boasted five-star nightclubs and hotels. Its nightlife rivaled Las Vegas with live music, plenty of shops, clubs, hotels, expensive cars, and lots of men and women with lots and lots of money. The only difference between the Miami strip and the Vegas strip is the beach! I was eleven miles from being right smack in the middle of it all. I went from the trailer park to Palm Beach to Miami Beach. It was my destiny to ride the wave!

It wasn't long until I felt right at home. I made sure I had an ample supply of white candy and made a special stop for a new little black book. I had a plan and couldn't wait for the weekend. Mr. Palm Beach gave me the tour and my instructions. There were two dozen apartments to rent in this building and I knew exactly who and what types of people he wanted. I was given keys to my own apartment and a Jaguar as a perk. I was off and running with one goal in mind: money and men.

Stripped of Shame

I started to scout the strip making my rounds. I made friends with bartenders. I repeated this venture week after week and so they could get used to my face. I became a regular. One night I was standing in the bar having a drink and I spotted this man making his way over to me.

"I haven't seen you here before," he said.

I acted completely unimpressed and replied, "Yeah, so?"

After a brief pause, he smiled and offered to buy me a drink. This guy didn't seem like some ordinary man. There was something very different about him. I agreed and we headed over to the bar. I noticed how the bartenders were quickly attentive to his every move. He had his own table and his own servers. After some small talk, he asked if I would take a ride with him to a grand opening of his new bar that was only a few blocks over. I didn't believe him at first, but since he was buying and there was something different about him, I agreed to go. We climbed into his Monte Carlo and he drove off.

The bar was just a few blocks away from the bar we met in. There was a line half a mile long of people waiting to get inside. The security and bouncers were resolutely standing in front of them, holding the thick red ropes securely, and kept everyone at bay. We pulled up in front of the bar and were greeted by the valet. Once we got close to the door, a massive man with big bulging muscles greeted us and ordered the other bouncers to pull back the ropes and let us in. I was very impressed. Once we got in the bar, my new friend was greeted by the waitresses, the bartenders, and all the security. Everyone knew him! I noticed a circle of men in fine suits and the band on the stage readying their instruments.

One of the bartenders instantly focused on us. I was told to order whatever I wanted. I made the decision that this was where I would make my home. This new friend of mine would be my ticket to freedom.

The beach was so beautiful, especially first thing in the morning. The luxuries were beyond what I could have ever imagined. My life had taken an immediate turn for the better since moving to Miami. Not only was I working alongside Mr. Palm Beach, but Mr. Miami, too. I was entwined in two kingdoms with two very powerful men. Mr. Palm Beach was my gateway into the elite, whereas Mr. Miami was the gateway to all the resources I needed to supply those elite. It wasn't too long after meeting Mr. Miami that I found myself living in the penthouse of his high-rise condominium. I liked to look out over the balcony and see South Beach and the stretch of water that bordered it.

Keeping my commitments to Mr. Palm Beach, I got right to work. Apartments were being rented and the women were coming and going. Money was flowing in like a sweet river. Meanwhile, I personally set my attention on nurturing my new found relationship with Mr. Miami and his world. I used my days to manage my new apartment-renting venture, but my late afternoons and evenings were spent in his club or at his penthouse. In no time I became known as Mr. Miami's girlfriend on the strip. I enjoyed the preferential treatment I experienced. I felt like a queen. When I reflected on my rough start of running away from life's tragedies and operating a small-time drug ring from the trailer park, Dede, who had become CC, was making it. I was going from penthouse to penthouse and driving a beautiful white Jaguar. I was finally getting everything she had lusted for back when vengeance became my motivation for living. I was living large and life was finally paying me back. I envied these two powerful men. My evil mind and corrupted soul edged on working on devising new ways to manipulate to get what I believed I really deserved. The power I wanted would be equal to theirs, at first and then even more. I became obsessed. Money and cocaine were merely the bridge to what my heart truly needed to accomplish retribution and that was having power over people. My passions took over and life became automatic. I juggled my businesses with the elites, kept up with people at the strip club, all the while nurturing my new relationship with Mr. Miami.

I had been burning the candle at both ends, which wasn't unusual, but it had been several months of keeping up with these two kingdoms when I started feeling the effects of little sleep and way too much play. I was both physically and mentally tired. I had reached the point of exhaustion. I became weary. The next thing I knew, my old enemy loneliness came knocking, and with it, depression. Those horrible memories returned, seeping in like the dripping of a leaky roof in a rainstorm. My thoughts advised me that I was no more in power than that of a slave and these two men I was involved with were using me to fulfill their sick lusts. The draw in my chest began pulling as the feelings of powerlessness and helplessness reached up like tentacles to embrace my soul. There was only one way I knew how to stop this: break out my old trusty friend and saviors: cocaine and alcohol. My emotions were getting the best of me. I wished I could turn back time and become a little girl again before all this happened. Without warning, the silent pull of death whispered in my ear.

I had to get away. I needed rest and wanted to be around someone who didn't want drugs. I desperately craved some normalcy, even if it was only for a weekend. I headed to West Palm Beach to hang out with an old friend who didn't know the extent of my businesses. We planned to order pizza and watch a movie, but sadly, half way through the movie I started getting restless. My body and mind needed its usual fix of cocaine and alcohol. I hadn't really acknowledged my addiction, since I was the dealer and religiously stuck to my cardinal rule. I always made sure to have my own stash. I headed for the bathroom and did a few lines. I enjoyed some small talk with my sweet friend and then excused myself and headed to the nearest bar. While still fighting the demons in my mind, I was approached by a man who asked me if I was Mr. Miami's girlfriend. Paranoia set in. I was in a bar I had never been in before, minding my own business, and was approached by someone who apparently knew me. I was suddenly frightened and I knew I had to get out of there.

I left my drink and blew this guy off. I immediately left the bar. I couldn't help but look out my review mirror the whole time I was driving. Terror gripped the inside of me at the thought of someone hurting me or abruptly ending my life as I knew it. I considered cutting back on the business or possibly giving it up all together, but this would almost be impossible to do. I was on the inside with some serious dealers and knew too much to get out of the game completely. I knew those personal vows I made back when this all started were still driving me. Before I really knew what I was doing I called my ex.

Within three days, he was at my door. The moment I saw him, all those memories flooded my heart. Oddly enough, we were very happy to see each other. Underneath that smile, he had an underlying agenda. That was the connection he and I had. It was as if we could read each other's mind and spirits. We were soul mates of darkness filled with lust and obsession. I returned to my apartment and proudly showed him how well I had made it without him. I handed him a plate with a large pile of cocaine and a straw. Within a few short hours, we were both back to our old habits. We were high as kites. Before I realized it, I had dived into more than my stash. I was breaking my cardinal rule. Twenty hours had come and gone and the sun was rising again. My beeper was blowing up and I was too ashamed to pick it up and respond. I had gone through all of my stash and dipped heavily into my product. I had the money to replenish what I took, but I went against my own rules and felt like such a fool.

Once again, the shame I felt had no mercy. I felt trapped. I realized that this fight was a lifelong one and my strength had faded. I still felt so empty. I still felt worthless, abandoned, and unhappy. I still felt unlovable and like I wasn't good enough. It didn't matter what I had done, how hard I had worked, or how kind I tried to be. The guilt overwhelmed me, the fear made me want to hide, and I started drowning. I needed out.

Another sunrise came and went. It was around the fourth day when he decided he wanted to leave Florida and return home. He asked me to go with him. Everything inside of me told me not to go, but I was in such a vulnerable state of mind. I agreed to go. I needed my world to stop and for it to be quiet, but most of all I needed my brother, my safe place.

That night, my ex and I jumped into the car Mr. Palm Beach allowed me to use. We had a couple of ounces of cocaine as headed towards the highway. I was so high and so lost. We were just about out of cocaine by the time we reached New York City. We stopped in his old neighborhood to meet up with some of his buddies he kicked around with. He took off and when he returned, he had an ounce of cocaine on him. I was so happy he scored. A couple of hits later, we were back on the highway headed further north. We made several stops along the way to rest and continued to devour the cocaine. I had no idea what I was doing, but I knew at some point I would need to come down and straighten up. Once again, the cocaine was running out and I was so far away from my home and my connections. Regret ripped through me like a tornado. Fear gripped my heart and paranoia paralyzed me. I needed my drug, especially if I was going to make it back to Florida. I was so terrified.

The cocaine was finally gone and we were like zombies driving into the sunrise. Being so drained from doing so much for so long, I sat in that passenger seat transfixed on the beauty of the skyline. The sunrise was always so beautiful to me. There was something so special about it.   Then, as if being awakened from a dream, the sounds of sirens abruptly shook me into reality. We were being pulled over by several police cars that had been tailing us. We pulled over and sat in the Jaguar waiting. I think I stopped breathing. I was so terrified. I had been up for days and was just coming down off the last bit of cocaine we had. The cops had their guns pulled and aimed directly at us. I was cuffed, thrown into the back of the cop car, and taken to jail. My charge was Grand Theft Auto. I spent the next couple of weeks in jail. By the beginning of the third week, I decided to call Mr. Miami. I needed help and I didn't have anyone else to call. I most certainly wasn't going to call my mother or father, not after the last time when they bonded me out. Thankfully Mr. Miami agreed to help, but with one condition. When I agreed, the very next day I had an immediate court hearing. The charges were dropped, no record shown, and I was released that afternoon.

After being released from jail, I found my way back home. I didn't move in with my parents. I ended up moving in with a neighbor two doors down. It was difficult to try to reconnect with my family. I had done so much damage by this point that trying to be a mother and daughter was foreign. I still hadn't figured out who I was. I was still so lost. It wasn't long until I headed back to what I knew. I went back to the bar scene, but things were not the same. The crowd was different and it felt like I had walked into a whole new era. I quickly met this girl who reminded me of me. She carried herself well and everyone knew she had the power. She had the drugs. She and I connected and I started running with her here and there, but nothing was really the same. There were so many new faces and new people to meet and trust. This was a much younger crowd. There were no loyalties. I was at the end of my game. I knew it, but I didn't know how to do anything else. I didn't know how to connect with the real world. I had been dealing drugs and calling my own shots since I was sixteen. I hadn't been trained to deal with society. In fact I was terrified of the real world. The truth was finally hitting me right in the face. I tried to ignore all that inner dialogue with myself, but somewhere inside of me I knew it was true. It was the end for me. Reality was about to hit.

I was charged with trafficking cocaine. I was cuffed and taken to jail. Life as I knew it was over. When I appeared in court, I couldn't believe my eyes. My father was there ready to bond me out. I was released to him and had to come back at a later date for my final sentencing. When I think back how I desperately needed help when I was a child, I needed help even more so as an adult. I was in real trouble.

I was looking at five years prison time, but the judge handed me time served with five years probation under these conditions: get a job, obtain a residence, and regain custody of my son. If I failed, I was guaranteed five years in prison. I was being offered a second chance and I knew it. I knew I needed a change. I needed to learn how to live a normal life. Without another thought, I signed all the paperwork and walked out of that courtroom so relieved. I couldn't believe the experiences I had lived through in such a short time of my life. I was such a lucky girl.

The Unexpected

After my life changing accident, I had to wait a few months to finalize the settlement. I was still trying to physically recover. I visited a bookstore looking for self-help books. A part of me wanted to prove that psychiatrist wrong. I refused to accept that I had been diagnosed with bi-polar disorder and deemed socially unacceptable. When I searched through the bookstore, I stumbled across books that promised that I could harness my own power to create my own destiny. This was exactly what I had been trying to do for so long. It only made sense that I buy the book and study it thoroughly. The book talked about inner power and untapped wells.

I devoured that book and returned to the bookstore scanning the aisles for more of the same. There were tons of books on tapping into your own power and the power of the air. My life didn't really change, but my perspective began to change. I felt a little happier. Those thoughts of death that visited me regularly were subsiding and I dove deeper into the study of new age books. I eventually bought a set of tarot cards.

I bypassed the Ouija board because some time ago one of my neighbors introduced the board to me. When I laid my fingertips on the center game piece that lay on the board, it began to float around the board by itself spelling out my name. It freaked me out because I had not moved that piece. It floated to letters around the board by itself. That was enough for me. I jumped up and told her no thanks. I was out of her house in seconds.

I did find the tarot cards interesting and learned a bit on meditation and chanting which seemed to be helping. These things were keeping me busy and I felt like I had found something that would help me change, get better, be smarter, and not be so afraid. Even though I found relief from the mental anguish, that relief didn't last long. I still suffered from severe flare ups from fibromyalgia that ran through my body. It made me feel like I was literally on fire and burning up. I was so thin and sickly looking, but thanks to the medication, I hadn't noticed it. Waiting for the settlement to be over was daunting. It was taking so long and I started to think it was pointless because of all the diagnosis the doctors spoke over me. I started wondering how the money could change that. I was still so broken, but now not only was I broken from the inside, I was broken on the outside too. For me, my life was essentially over. I was hopeless.

The constant heartache of all the poor choices I made in my life haunted me. I felt so helpless. *My dad was right, I was a fool. I should have known better. Why didn't I listen? It was truly all my fault!* I closed myself up in my room and reviewed my list of failures over and over again. I made the decision to kill myself. I would eat all my pills, gulp down all the beer I had in my refrigerator, and go quietly to sleep. If I couldn't find peace, I would go to sleep escaping the pain and peace would find me. Suddenly there was a knock on my bedroom window. It was a buddy of mine.

I opened the front door and the first thing he said was, "Wow, you look like shit!" He then asked if I wanted to go to the beach. He told me he took the day off. I figured I could hang with him for the day and finish my plan that evening. He waited while I put on my bathing suit and grabbed a towel. Then we headed out to the beach.

I sat facing the ocean. I imagined what it would be like to go out as far as I could and never return. What would it be like to be completely and utterly free? My friend Timothy was facing in the opposite direction and was preoccupied with rolling a joint. He had no idea of my intense inner turmoil. I had not told him of my plans to take my own life.

I lay there with my thoughts drifting in and out with the waves. Suddenly I noticed a man jogging down the beach looking in my direction. There was another man dressed in what looked like a white bathrobe walking directly to his right. The jogger intently returned my gaze and made me feel as though he was not looking at me. I felt as though he was looking through me. I continued my defiant stare back, but wondered why the stranger seemed so interested in me.

His intense gaze and now broadening smile continued as he passed directly in front of me. He didn't feel threatening. He looked rather inexplicably sweet and gentle. Though I did not return his smile when he was at his nearest, I did immediately envision the pictures of Jesus I had seen hung throughout my home as a kid.

I turned to my buddy and said "Timothy, check out this guy jogging down the beach. He looks just like Jesus!" When we both looked back up, the jogger and his walking buddy were nowhere to be seen. The two of us looked to the left and to the right, but the jogger and his walking friend were nowhere in sight. After swearing up and down I saw what I saw, we decided to let it go.

We spent a couple of hours on the beach. When we stopped for lunch, I had the opportunity to let it all out. I expressed to my sweet friend how the pain and turmoil I was hanging onto was consuming me. He didn't say too much. He just listened intently. As we were leaving the restaurant, I threw him the keys and asked him to drive. We were heading back to his place when he said to me, "Dede, you know what your problem is? You don't have any faith."

"Faith? What's that?" I replied.

He said, "You just don't believe in anything."

Up to that point I had never even heard of faith.

There was an awkward silence during the rest of the drive to his place. The word faith permeated me somehow. I mulled it over the whole drive. We pulled up to his apartment and he turned and asked if I wanted him to come home with me. I politely turned him down, considering I still had something I wanted to do. I thanked him for the morning and jumped back into the driver's seat.

Stripped of Shame

I didn't give the word faith anymore thought while driving home. The loneliness returned knowing I was headed home to an empty apartment with death on my mind. I remained in my car for a few extra minutes in my driveway. Then with much trepidation, I slowly opened the car door and got out of the car.

When I got home, I fumbled with my keys by the front door. I suddenly heard my mother's voice in my head. It was the voice she used when she would tell me I needed Jesus and that I needed to watch the Christian channel. I didn't even know what channel the Christian channel was. At that moment, I heard an audible voice speak the numbers "Four-six." I had no idea what was going on, but as soon as I got through my front door, I reached down for the remote. I hit the power button and turned to channel forty-six. To my surprise, there were people talking about Jesus. I threw the remote down and sat on the couch.

I couldn't comprehend anything the people on television were saying. It all sounded like a foreign language to me, but I kept watching. I don't recall how much time went by, but I didn't forget the plans I had made earlier that morning. I grabbed my bottle of painkillers from my room and the six-pack of beer I had in my refrigerator.

I opened the pill bottle and popped open a beer. I threw a few painkillers in my mouth and chased it with the brew. I listened to a man talk on the television about how he was supposed to die because he was diagnosed with a tumor in his brain and didn't have much time to live, but God healed him. He immediately caught my attention because of his uncanny resemblance to my deceased brother. I sat back transfixed. He was wearing an all-white suit, the same color suit we laid my brother to rest in. My pulse began to race and my heart pounded with grief. I readied myself to go through with the suicide.

In the precise moment I grabbed the pill bottle to raise to my mouth, the man on the television screamed out, "You are healed, in Jesus' name!" In an instant, my foot that was injured in the automobile accident began to tingle. My big toe began to tingle. My foot began to have feeling. I couldn't deny that something beyond me and my experience was happening. I dropped the pill bottle and the beer bottle and stood up and like someone trying on a new pair of shoes, I walked around my living room, down to my bedroom, and back through the living room feeling out my foot. When it was obvious that there was real feeling there, I started screaming out "I can feel my foot! I have feeling in my foot!"

I made my way into the kitchen and pulled out a fork. I poked at my foot to test it. There was feeling for sure. The doctors told me that I would never again have feeling in that foot because of the deep nerve damage, so how could I suddenly have feeling in it? Still a little doubtful, I pulled out a sharp knife and poked at it. I could feel the sharpness. I don't remember smiling so big in a really long time. It had been so long since I felt anything remotely like joy or happiness. *Could there be hope for me? Could this be what hope feels like?*

It was just after midnight when I decided to call my mother. "What's wrong?" she asked.

I replied, "Mom, I can feel my foot! I was watching the Christian channel and this guy said I was healed, and I can feel my foot!"

Stripped of Shame

She thought I was completely crazy, so she just said "Good, good." She would talk to me in the morning.

I hung up and walked around my house screaming out, "I have feeling in my big toe! I have feeling in my big toe!" Joy positively erupted out of me. I realized I had a broad smile on my face, testifying that something wonderful had happened inside also. For the first time in what seemed like forever, I was happy. I could feel my big toe and my foot. Something had come to life in me and it had started with my big toe.

That night was special in so many ways. The fact that I didn't go through with my suicide plan was miraculous enough, but I had also experienced God's love for me without knowing it was God. His love opened a portal of hope when I was at my end and saved me.

While I cleaned up the mess on the coffee table and off the floor, I kept the television on. I listened intently to a man hosting a program where he encouraged people to call in for prayer. The callers would call in and share their situation and ask for prayer for themselves or others. The very last caller was a woman who shared in detail her life experiences. The more she shared, the more I saw myself in her story. I was stunned by the sheer improbability of it all. I thought to myself, *"This woman is me!" I wondered how she knew to call for prayer, while I didn't." What was it about prayer that someone would call a local TV station and share their personal experiences on the air anyway? Didn't she find that embarrassing?* I listened with intense anticipation as they prayed. Something inside me was moved to pray too. It was certainly unfamiliar, but somehow it felt right. After they were finished praying I turned the television off and went to bed. I remember turning the hall light on, an old habit that started because of the boogie man and his buddies I saw in the night. But something was slightly different this night, and for the first time in a very long time, I didn't keep my bedroom light burning. This was another minor miracle. I crawled into bed still trying to come to grips with the day's events. I was hopeful, although that state of mind was so foreign to me. I wasn't sure if hope was really what I was experiencing, but I felt different.

That night I had such a vivid dream. When I awoke, it was difficult to tell if the dream was a dream or if something actually happened. I dreamt I saw a lamb walk into my room, climb into my bed, and snuggle up gently against my back. It was so real. It was as if this white lamb guarded me throughout the entire night allowing me to sleep in peace. I laid there in my bed a few more minutes mulling over the dream when I remembered my foot. I threw the covers off and eased my way out of bed. I could still feel my foot. I noticed the heaviness that usually greeted me each morning wasn't there. I was actually smiling from the inside.

I made my way to the kitchen for my usual coffee, cigarettes, and pain meds. Before I could take my morning shower, my mother showed up at my door. While I was sharing with her all that had happened, there was another knock at my door. It was Timothy. I started sharing with both of them in detail what happened the night before. I showed them my big toe. My mother shared in the excitement with me. Meanwhile Timothy elaborated on my dream. He tried to explain something about Jesus being the Lamb of God. I didn't understand anything he was saying, but he certainly was smiling big as he was trying to tell me about Jesus and this lamb thing.

The next couple of days were filled with Christian television shows. My nights continued to be peaceful. One morning while watching, I had such a strong feeling to get on my knees and pray, so I did. I turned the television off and hit the floor. That morning I cried out to God in heartfelt prayer. I didn't really know how to pray or what to say, I just spoke out. "God, I don't know you, but whatever you have I want. Please help me, I can't help myself."

After that simple prayer, I started crying. These tears came in a torrent born from a life of pain, loss, and betrayal. Like the snowpack melting in the mountains in springtime, my heart was softening. I cried for three solid days. I cried in the shower, on the toilet, in the kitchen cooking, while I cleaned, and while I sat. I didn't know it then, but not all those tears were tears of sadness for a misspent life. They were tears of release, liberation, and joy.

The morning of the fourth day, I awoke with a sudden and intense urge to read a Bible. I had never read one before, so after my shower, I got dressed and headed out to purchase a Bible. I was amazed at what I read. The words were positively jumping up and out at me. Here in the pages of this book, I began to experience liberation unlike anything I have ever experienced before. I tore through the pages of that Bible like a starving animal. There were times I would loudly exclaim, "That's so true!" I was awestruck with the practicality of what I read.

Doreen Stumpf

After a couple days of voraciously reading the Bible, something inside me came to an immediate stop. What was alive immediately became cold and I hit a wall. I didn't know what was happening. I wondered if I had done something wrong. Was this the end? I got up and wandered aimlessly around my apartment. I felt unsettled. I didn't understand the promptings of the Holy Spirit at that time. I stood silently in the middle of my bedroom. My eyes wandered directly to the shrine I had built when I was studying those self- help books. I had a collection of candles, dead flowers, and handwritten incantations. I walked over to it and began to dismantle it. I tore things down and walked it out the back door. I pulled out my large metal trash can and threw everything into it. I scoured my apartment and grabbed all the books, tarot cards, candles, dead flowers, oils, incense, incantations, and pictures and threw everything into the trash can.

I tore down all the blankets I had tacked up behind my curtains that blocked out sunlight. I went from room to room, window to window, and tore those darkening blankets down. All of it went into the trash. I pulled out the cleaner and disinfected the bathroom, wiped down window sills and baseboards, and used Windex for the windows now filled with rays of beautiful sunlight. I polished the furniture, vacuumed the carpets, and mopped my small kitchen. Within a couple of hours, I had cleansed my entire six hundred square foot apartment.

When I finally felt finished, I stood in my backyard and stared at the full trash can. I looked over to my left and conveniently noticed a red plastic jug labeled gasoline. Without a second thought, I sprinkled enough in the can to start a nice little fire. I stepped back, lit a match, and threw it in. Flames consumed a small part of my hopeless past. That day my curiosity of new age philosophy and the discovery of my own inner power were brought together in a metal trash can and burned.

I was hungry for God. I wanted to know as much as I could about Jesus and by this time I was convinced He rescued me at my darkest and lowest point. I had gone to the beach that day with my buddy Tim looking and hoping for nothing. Jesus had gone to the beach that day looking for me and found me. Jesus lit a flame in me that day and the flame He lit caused me to want to know His love for me.

Each day felt like a new day. I had an unexplainable hunger to learn who Jesus was. I didn't mind hearing it from other people or the television ministers, but since I carried so much distrust toward people, I needed to get to know Jesus myself.

One day while reading and studying the Bible, there was a knock at my front door. I wasn't expecting anyone, so it caught me off guard. When I opened the door, there stood a cable technician who said that he had received a call for my address. I had called no one and there was nothing wrong with my cable, so I assumed he had the wrong address and told him so. As we tried to figure out where the error was in his work order, he overheard the television evangelist talking about Jesus. That led to a conversation about God.

One thing led to another and he opened up about his life. I couldn't believe my ears. Once again, I found myself hearing someone else's story which was incredibly similar to mine. I invited him inside and took a seat on my couch. Tears began to well up in my eyes. His words seem to pierce through me. It was hardly a normal conversation one has with a cable technician. After a few moments, he knelt and in all apparent sincerity told me he was Job like the man Job from the Bible. He identified with him in a sense. The story in the Book of Job tells about a man who was tested and tried, lost everything, then was told by his friends that he was losing his mind, and was probably even in rebellion toward God. But in the end, he regained double for all that had been taken from him.

I had the strangest feeling that this was no accident. He rose up and started to walk toward the front door, gave me a broad smile, and said, "Hang in there." The smile had something behind it and was incredibly similar to the smile of the jogger on the beach. He opened the door, crossed the threshold, and turned his head and looked right at me, and said, "Have a nice day." He then shut the door behind him.

Was I just visited by an angel? I had to find a church, I had to find out more of this Jesus and I needed someone to teach me, but where would I begin? How does one go about finding a church? My only experience with church was the Catholic school I was enrolled in as a child in my elementary years before moving to Florida. In what little experience I had seeking God, I don't recall hearing much about Jesus. Lacking any knowledge of denominations or theological creeds, I decided to go back to what I knew. I would attend the nearest Catholic Church.

The alarm went off early the following Sunday morning. I got up and put on one of my favorite sundresses and slipped into my flip-flops. I grabbed my purse and keys and headed out to church. I was a little nervous because I would be returning to the church that I walked into a few years earlier and defiled it by my bad attitude and behavior. I was also excited that now I would be returning with the Bible in hand to learn more of Jesus. Walking through the parking lot, I immediately noticed how everyone was dressed. At first, I didn't feel embarrassed. People looked at me and smiled, so I didn't think anything of it. After all, I was seeking Jesus and assumed that was their intention, too. After Mass, they gathered in an adjoining building for punch and snacks. I was excited to meet other people who also know Jesus. I thought they were probably a better crowd than the people I used to hang with on Sunday mornings.

People were gathered around tables eating muffins and drinking coffee. Moments later, a woman stood to welcome everyone and asked if anyone had questions, I raised my hand, but she overlooked me. She chose another person who had their hand raised and answered their question. She asked "Anyone else?" I raised my hand and once again she overlooked me. I felt that pang in my heart and my cheeks beginning to flush with shame. A few more minutes went by and a few other people asked their questions. She politely addressed them. Meanwhile, I defiantly kept my arm up. She finally directed her gaze towards me and made a sarcastic comment regarding my clothing in front of everyone. I looked around and noticed everyone staring at me. In that moment, that old shame that I hadn't felt in some time returned. I felt so humiliated. I immediately grabbed my purse, picked up my Bible, and left. By the time I walked all the way through the parking lot and back to my car, I was in tears.

A few days later, still determined to find someone to teach me about Jesus, I called the office of that same church and made an appointment to meet with the priest. I would make sure to dress appropriately to protect myself from further ridicule. I pulled open those heavy doors, entered, and took a seat in the foyer. I remember it being dark and really cold. The receptionist came out and asked if she could help me. I told her I had an appointment to meet with the priest. It took a few minutes before he came walking down a long corridor and invited me back to his office. He offered me a seat and asked how he might help me. I told him I just found Jesus and I wanted to know more about Him. While he did speak some vague generalities, he mostly spoke of the church service times, what was expected of congregants, and the various available activities. He never told me about Jesus. He abruptly rose from his chair, held his hand towards the door, and said, "Here let me show you out." Our conversation was obviously over.

I followed beside him as we made our way back up that long dark corridor towards the foyer. He pushed open the big heavy doors for me and told me it was important to show up for Mass on Sunday and not to worry about reading the Bible. He said that he would tell me all I needed to know.

I left angry and very disappointed. I made my way back to the car, slammed the door shut, and started the engine. *Who was going to help me? How was I going to find out about Jesus?* My search began anew in the most ordinary way. I used the Yellow Pages. I was out to find a church that was similar to the teachings of Joyce Meyer. I had been consistently watching her and needed to find a fellowship that made the Bible not only practical, but also understandable. I began my perusal through the telephone book, calling one church after another. I asked whoever answered if they taught like Joyce Meyer. Many had never heard of her and others said that there were no such churches in the area. With my frustration mounting, I decided to call one more church. I closed my eyes and my finger landed on Faith Family Church.

The pastor's wife answered the phone. We spoke for nearly two hours. The whole time we conversed, she told me of Jesus and His love. The hairs on my arms were literally standing at attention. She said they knew of Joyce Meyer and the church's teachings paralleled hers. She understood what it meant to be in pursuit of Jesus, of wanting to know more about Him, and how to study the Bible. The entire time I was on the telephone, excitement and joy rose up in me. We ended our conversation with her telling me the times of the Sunday services. She left me with a sincere invitation to attend. I couldn't wait until Sunday!

I turned the alarm off and I rolled out of bed with a sense of joy. I wondered if wearing the same attire that had drawn the collective scorn of the Catholic Church would be a good idea. I thought about it a bit more over coffee and decided that I would wear the same outfit as a test. I believed that their reaction to me would tell me more than any sermon or theological debate ever could. When I walked through those doors that morning, to my delight, I was welcomed with hugs, smiles, and acceptance. Their style of service wasn't anything I had ever experienced. It was very non-traditional. I felt comfortable and made a decision that I would come back again the next Sunday.

This new way of living brought me new friends. These new friends were also seeking a relationship with Jesus, which encouraged me to keep going. A few months went by and I actually felt like I belonged somewhere. I started to attend more than just on Sunday mornings. I started going on Wednesday nights and when the Church offered a correspondence course, I signed up. The classes met three times a week and I was getting more of Jesus than your average churchgoer. That faith thing my friend Timothy talked about was making its way into my heart and I was really starting to understand it. I learned how to study the Bible, how to interpret scriptures, and how to understand the will of God.

Classes were great. One day while sitting in class, I felt something lift off of me and leave my body. I sat there mesmerized, frozen, not knowing what just happened. Then I noticed that I didn't feel the chronic pain of fibromyalgia radiating through me. My mind was trying so hard to put to words what just happened. I excused myself to the ladies room. It was very much like what happened to my big toe and foot. *Was God healing me little by little?*

I was still so new to Christianity. I seemed to learn things by experience first, then found confirmation in the Bible afterwards. I remember the day I was puzzled about who to pray to. Was it to God, Jesus, or the Holy Spirit? I took the question to my pastors. They told me to pray to all of them, for they are one. That is what the trinity is: the Father, the Son, and the Holy Spirit. They were so pleased to see how much I had grown in such a short period of time. In my first year of Bible school, I had been caught up in a love affair with Jesus. His intense love for me was waking me up. I was coming alive. My heart was coming alive. I had faith!

Things were going well for me. My body was feeling better and the fibromyalgia didn't return. There were no more flair ups or pain. My big toe and foot had full feeling. I started to just know things. My church offered a second year of Bible school. I signed up and began to go deeper. The second year taught me so much more of God as we studied the Old Testament and how it was a shadow of Jesus who was to come in the New Testament. I was popping with all kinds of revelations of Father God, Jesus His son, and the Holy Spirit. I was learning about the Kingdom of God. It was so cool!

Halfway through the second year, I noticed other areas of my life that weren't so easy to overcome. The debilitating grief over the death of my brother still caused me pain. Even though I was making great progress in several other areas, this was a spiritual millstone around my neck. I was still so angry that my only brother, whom I had loved so much, had been taken from me. I was advised the best way to deal with this was to seek out all the scriptures I could find on joy and read them out loud. Reading out loud helped me hear what the Word of God said about having joy. I searched out scriptures and read them over and over. I did this for a time and it didn't seem to really help. It felt like this pain ran so much deeper. This wasn't like the healing of my foot.

119

Doreen Stumpf

I was still taking medication for pain in my lower back and by this time I had a full blown addiction to opiates. When these episodic moments came about, I would take more medication than prescribed. I would feel horrible and start to lose focus on all the good things that were happening. It almost felt as though the honeymoon state of this new life and adventure was fading and that I was doomed to go backwards. This faith stuff was becoming more of a fight to keep than in the beginning. My realities were getting larger again and the real pain of loss revisited me.

One Sunday morning I awoke with such a burden on my heart. The grief was back. Why did it keep coming back? It was too heavy to carry, so I ended up staying home from church thinking it would help if I just spent the morning reading and praying. I made my coffee, downed some medicine, and sat down. I was about an hour or so into my study time when all of a sudden, frustration came over me. Without a second thought, I threw my Bible across the room. I paced the apartment, lit one cigarette after another, and felt my anger and sense of loss mount like a prairie thunderstorm. I looked at the television and a woman preacher was on the screen. At that precise moment she said, "God is coming for that thing; that thing that is holding you in bondage!" It felt as though she was speaking right to me. I walked over to my couch and sat down. This pain was so familiar. It was the same rageful anger and pain I felt the day I decided to drive to the church and tell God just how angry I was.

In the midst of that anger and heart wracking pain, I felt the Holy Spirit of God prompting me.

Stripped of Shame

With some resistance, I walked up the stairs to my bedroom. Taking my time, I grabbed a blanket to lie on the floor and neatly straightened it out before I sat on it. As I was straightening out one final corner of the blanket, I felt something press upon my back, which literally caused me to collapse onto my knees and lay on my belly. The moment I was in this position, I began to cry.

The intensity of my emotional outburst took me by surprise. It wasn't a soft, weepy sort of release but one of great pain. The sobs came forth in floods. I let out screams that sounded like agony. Even though my eyes were shut, I became aware of a man standing in front of me. In my mind's eye, I was lying at His feet. I saw His sandals and the hem of His white robe. My release continued, all the while my Savior stood with me. He healed, comforted, and delivered me.

When it was all over, I crawled into my bed. Lying there alone, emptied of the burden of the death of my brother, I drifted off to sleep. I awoke sometime later and remembered what I believe was a dream. The dream seemed as if I was awake. I saw myself in a casket. I was alive, yet I was dead. I didn't understand the dream at the time. I believe Jesus showed up to start the healing process in the deeper parts of my broken heart. My heart was terribly wounded, confused, and hurt. Once again Jesus met me in the deepest parts of my painful heart, bringing freedom in such a way that could only be explained as a miracle. I believe to this day that He allowed me to experience a new birth in Him by awakening the girl who died with her brother that day.

Georgia Bulldog... Just Do It!

I had pretty much separated completely from my old life. I still missed my ex-boyfriend, but he and I were not headed in the same direction. I had fallen in love with Jesus, so I chose Jesus and left. I received the settlement from the truck accident and was settled in my church. I had developed some solid relationships, particularly with the pastor's mother. She was a huge help in encouraging me to stick with Jesus every time I thought I made a mistake leaving my boyfriend. Those times were hard. One day in my grief over this separation, I had an experience where I felt as if somehow in the spirit, God helped me to separate fully. I remember literally feeling something pulling away from me like it was being torn off me. As I continued to experience these intermittent miracles, I remembered visualizing strips of Velcro being peeled apart.

Around the time I was finishing up the second year of Bible school, a new couple started attending our church. I got to know them pretty well. They had children who were around the same age as my son. My new found friend, Ruth, explained that she believed God impressed upon her that she and her family were to move next door to me. We spent nearly two years as neighbors and attended the same church.

Having her right next door really helped, especially when I suffered setbacks. There were days I wanted to quit following Jesus. There were days I would have a tantrum and burst out in a rage. There were times I didn't understand and would grab my purse and head to the store for alcohol. But through it all, Jesus was there and He made sure to move someone right next door who would be there, too.

One day Ruth came over to tell me that God had put it on her and her husband's heart to move to Cumming, Georgia and help a women's recovery ministry called Abba House. The news nearly killed me. She had mentioned this place to me before, but I never gave it much thought. She and her husband knew the founders pretty well. They had lived with them at one time. You can see how she felt that moving to North Georgia made sense. It was a sad goodbye for me and my son, because for the first time in a long time, I had a friend and my son had regular visitors on a daily basis. Now the whole family would be leaving. On the day that they left, I sat on my front porch. Tears welled up in my eyes as I watched their U-Haul truck drive away. I was alone again and although my precious son was with me, I couldn't seem to get over feeling like I had been punched in the stomach.

Stripped of Shame

It had been around two months since Ruth and her family moved when she called and invited me to visit. I had never been that far away from my family before, so this would prove to be a little challenging for me. Since I knew them and felt safe with them, I mapped out directions and planned a trip to North Georgia. It was very country and nothing like I'd ever experienced. I did enjoy driving along the mountains with its curvy roads. I looked at cows, horses, and chicken coops. She and her family looked like they were settling in pretty well. Monday rolled around and Ruth invited me to go with her to see the Abba House. When we got there, it wasn't anything like I thought it would be. I imagined a building with offices, similar to a residential hospital setting, but what I was looking at was a piece of land with a couple of cottages, a recently donated modular, and a small thrift store.

The residents in the program lived in the cottages. The modular was in the process of being renovated for new living space. The overall atmosphere was warm, friendly, and welcoming. It looked very much like a home would or should be. After being introduced to everyone, I shopped in the thrift store. She and I left around lunchtime. Unbeknownst to me, God was up to something.

The founders had dinner with all the women in the program every Monday night. They called it Sharp Night in honor of the founders Jim and Chris Sharp. It was a time to demonstrate what family and relationships looked like for those who may have never had experienced it. After dinner, we all went outside to enjoy a bonfire. I remember it being so cold. As a Floridian, I wasn't used to this kind of cold weather.

I needed to warm up, so I got up and walked over to the fire, but I couldn't get warm. I stepped over the logs that encircled the fire and stepped right into the bonfire pit itself and nestled my feet as close to the fire as I could without melting my tennis shoes. While I was standing there trying to get warm, I started feeling awkward. Emotions and feelings that I couldn't distinguish were rushing through me, but what was most unnerving was the thought that–I might end up at this Abba House place myself. In the moment of this mental battle, Jim Sharp, the founder, walked into the pit and stood right beside me.

"So when will you be coming to Abba House?" he asked. I just looked at him. With a gentle smile, he nodded his head and stepped back out.

I happened to be wearing the only sweat shirt I could find from shopping in the thrift store earlier that morning. It was a grey University of Georgia sweatshirt. "Georgia Bulldogs, Just Do It" was emblazoned across the front in dark red letters. When I bought it, I thought of my sweet friend from church who told me that I reminded her of a bulldog. She said "When you latch your teeth onto something Dede, you refuse to let go!" There I was in the fire pit wearing this sweatshirt with a bulldog and the words "just do it" on the front!

That night haunted me for the rest of my stay. I started feeling uneasy and I was so ready to head back home to Florida. The following night, Ruth invited a few women over to her house. The evening started out with small talk and food before everyone moved into the living room. Someone suggested we play a board game which made me feel rather anxious. I wasn't used to being around so many women in this type of environment. I went into the room where I had my things and took a pain pill to ease my fears. When I returned to the living room, Chris, Jim's wife and co-founder of Abba House, immediately asked me about my pain pill addiction. What I thought was just a friendly get-together was in fact an intervention.

I immediately became defensive. *It was none of their business. My life was none of their business.* I felt betrayed and humiliated, so I left the next morning. Ruth apologized over and over, explaining she only did what she did because she actually cared about me. Without a word, I walked out of her home and got in my car. I pulled out of her driveway planning to never speak to her again. The eight hour drive home gave me plenty of time to think. A part of me knew that what they were saying was true. I was a Christian with an addiction. I most certainly depended on the pain pills to get through life. I thought of how many times I had tried to stop, even for a day, and couldn't. The only way to reconcile this argument with myself was to focus on what the doctors told me. They were certain that I would need pain pills for the rest of my life because of the chronic pain in my lower back. I believed them, accepted it, and depended on it. When anyone challenged me, I would always use the doctor card.

I arrived home just in time to refill my prescription. I went an hour past my usual dosage time and withdrawal symptoms set in. I started feeling really anxious while I waited on my prescription at the pharmacy. As my heart raced when my name was finally called, I realized the ladies in North Georgia might be right. I was a Christian with an addiction. I was not relying on God to set me completely free. I couldn't imagine my life without pain pills. I needed my pain pills and my doctors. When I finally had the prescription in my hands, I ripped open the bag, unscrewed the top of the bottle, and hurriedly downed a few pills.

Guilt washed over me as I walked out of Wal-Mart. I knew that I needed help but I wasn't ready to accept any help just yet. Ruth hadn't stopped calling and eventually we were back on speaking terms. Between her and Jesus, it was only a matter of time before I was packing my bags and made the decision to return to Abba House. My son, now eighteen years old, decided to live with his father in hopes to restore and build on their relationship.

I spent Thanksgiving with my family. The evening before I left for Georgia, I almost backed out, but the guilt and shame I walked in continually pushed me to seek more of God. I didn't stop taking medication, but I knew Jesus loved me anyway. He showed me many things in His word as I sought out scripture daily. He didn't reject me because I couldn't stop smoking or taking pain pills and muscle relaxers. He stuck with me the entire time, loving me to life.

After saying goodnight to everyone I crawled into my bed. I still wasn't a hundred percent sure of what I was about to do, but the Spirit of God brought to my mind the day I sat with my dad and asked his thoughts on the matter. He had no knowledge of Abba House, nor did we really talk much about my new lifestyle. At one point he thought this was just a phase I was going through. I reached out to him and to my surprise, my dad said he thought it was a good idea and I should go.

God is so good! He was always doing little things to build on my confidence, ensuring I was hearing Him. This helped me become even more attentive to His Spirit. When the Spirit of God reminded me of that little moment with my father, it was as if He was saying to me, "It is going to be okay. Your father has given you his blessing and so have I."

As I snuggled into bed, I felt the gentle nudge from the Holy Spirit to pull out my now much-worn Bible and turn to Isaiah Chapter 43. My eyes fell immediately on verses eighteen and nineteen, which read,

"Forget the former things: Do not dwell on
the past. See, I am doing a new thing! Now
it springs up; do you not perceive it? I am
making a way in the wilderness and streams
in the wasteland."
New International Version

The anxiety I had disappeared. I closed my Bible, laid my head down, and slept. I was ready to go. I pulled out of my parents' driveway the next morning and headed towards the turnpike. Things were going well until I reached Atlanta. I got lost trying to find Georgia 400 and had to pull into a gas station to ask for directions. Standing next to an old pickup truck pumping gas, a man with shoulder length, sandy blonde hair, wearing blue jeans and a tee shirt smiled at me. As I got out of my car to head into the gas station, the man caught my attention by asking me if I was lost. I nodded yes and told him I needed to know how to get to Georgia 400. With a gentle smile and his ocean-blue eyes glistening in the sun, he pointed in the direction I should take and told me how to get on my way.

I jumped back in my car and headed in the direction he pointed me to. I was immediately on the right road. An overwhelming feeling of joy bubbled up from deep inside me. This joy wasn't shallow like the happiness when someone gives you a present on your birthday, this joy felt alive and intoxicating. My body actually tingled from the inside out. At that moment, I knew that the man who just gave me directions was no ordinary man. I believe that it was Jesus Himself helping me find the way.

Soon, I arrived safely in Cumming. Anxiety gripped me. I reached into my purse and pulled out a pain pill before pulling into Ruth's driveway. Memories of the last visit flooded my mind and I started doubting if this was God or something else drawing me here. I was in the same condition physically. My doctors had given me enough refills on my meds to last until I could find a local doctor. I had brought along my x-rays and doctor notes to prove to the staff that there was a real issue, and although I couldn't just stop taking the medication, I had reason not to. With their willingness to help, I was willing to give this Abba house thing a try.

My mind raced back and forth with thoughts of abandoning my family, my son, my new church, and everyone else I knew back in Florida. My once pathetic life started to not look so bad, especially now that I had given my life over to Jesus. When I thought of how I had given up my townhome, packed all my furniture into storage, and left family I'd start to panic. I felt angry. I was mainly angry at myself, but strangely enough, each time I thought about leaving and going against what I believed God was doing, something would stop me.

The first thirty days were so hard. I missed my son and family so much. I missed my home, my things, and especially my hometown. I started becoming convinced that I had made the biggest mistake ever. I still didn't have a real knowing of what God was up to behind this scene. I only knew that there were too many miracles that took place that could've only been God. I had to remind myself over and over how only God could have orchestrated my neighbor's daughter returning from the military pregnant and needing a place to live at the precise time I needed to break my lease. I recalled how my landlord was so favorable in allowing her to take over my lease with no complications and how U-Haul handed me free boxes and gave me a super deal to store my things. It seemed like people were randomly showing up to help me everywhere I went. They were super friendly, generous, and they were women!

It was after lunch on a blustery cold day when I and four other women gathered in the living room of the new modular. We were getting ready for group to start. The door opened and in came Jim to lead group. After a couple of songs and prayer, there was a time of silence. Then we all sat back down on the couches and group started. Jim had such an uncanny way of looking at people. He had such a deep piercing stare, that if you didn't know him, you might think he was angry at you. I was still considered a new resident and I was scared out of my wits.

One of the girls in the group started talking. "Jim, I'm struggling with hating my dad because of his violent behavior towards my mother, and how he treated me and my dog just as bad as he treated her. I loved my dog and my dad made me get rid of it."

I was less than compassionate. *Her dog? Are you kidding me? Give me a break!* I couldn't believe she was struggling over a memory of a dog.

The girl kept on talking about how much she cared for the dog and how she was able to connect with it because she never felt good enough to connect with anyone in her family. She found comfort knowing that her pet loved her unconditionally. As much as I thought that this was rather childish, I continued to pay close attention. She was asked how it made her feel that her father didn't care about how she felt about her dog. She said it made her feel like he really didn't care about how she felt. She was then asked when she first realized that her father didn't care about her feelings. She said she remembered watching them fight when she was five years old. That particular fight suddenly got out of control. She said her father turned around and yelled at her to grab the dog and go to her room. She said her father hated the dog and hated that she loved the dog and was later made to get rid of it. She started crying and stated that the dog was her only friend.

I started to freak out because I could relate to this girl's story. I remembered watching my parents fight when I was a young child. I had an Alaskan German Shepherd puppy and one day while I was at school, my father was busy. He left the backyard gate open and my puppy ran out into the street. My puppy was hit and killed by a car. I was eight years old.

Stripped of Shame

Her story revealed painful emotions in me. The problem was I didn't know how to react to this kind of emotion outside of getting angry and filled with rage. I noticed Jim turn and look at me. Perhaps he could sense the pressure building up in me. I'm sure I was turning colors. He turned his gaze back to the girl who was still crying. He asked if she would like to forgive her father for making her feel this way. She said yes. First he guided her in repenting for the judgments she held against her dad. One by one she repented for judging her dad for being insensitive, angry, abusive, and uncaring. Jim helped her pray to forgive her dad for those things and how he made her feel. She told him she swore she would never marry a man like her father, but her current husband was abusive, hard, and uncaring, and he didn't like dogs either.

Jim walked her through renouncing that oath by praying this prayer. "Lord, I renounce the vow I made that I would never marry a man like my father and I break that now in the name of Jesus. Forgive me Lord for making these vows and promises which I am unable to keep." Then he asked her what she believed about herself. She said she didn't believe she deserved anything good. Jim told her to ask God for the answer.

Her eyes were still closed in prayer, but mine were wide open. I was witness to a miracle of how Jesus heals the wounded heart and soul. Right before my eyes, her countenance was as bright as the sun. It was as if the weather outside went from bitter cold to a sweet summer day. God was showing me something here. He was introducing me to something new.

My mind started racing with questions. *What just happened?* Then as if he heard my thoughts, Jim turned his gaze to me.

"So, Doreen, what do you think about what just happened?" he asked.

"I'm not too sure," I replied, "but her story was very familiar. I'm just not ready to talk."

He respectfully smiled then moved on to another willing vessel who wanted to talk.

What did it all mean?

The next day after lunch, we all took our seats in the living room. Everyone got comfortable. I had been struggling with the thought of dredging up old memories. My church taught me to lay aside those things and look forward to the things ahead of me. There were scriptures to back it up. I sat there mulling these things over when the door opened. Jim, guitar in one hand, papers and his Bible in the other, walked in.

He handed out the papers to each of us. The lyrics of the songs we were about to sing were printed on them. We all stood up and began to sing. Again, I found myself watching, but not really participating. Jim offered a prayer of thanksgiving and took his seat. I felt so out of place.

We were asked to grab our Bibles and open to Genesis chapter 3, which talks about the fall of man. Jim discussed what he believed to be the classic human strongholds: shame, fear, and control. He continued to explain how these three strongholds are the culprits to our broken relationships. I sat there listening, but not really agreeing because of all the teaching I sat under through two years of Bible school. In my mind I had learned a thing or two. *How*

Stripped of Shame

in the world would anyone benefit from dealing with past pain that has caused shame, guilt, and fear? I had been taught to press on toward the things that were set before me, not look back on the things that were behind me.

It was difficult to wrap my head around having to deal with issues that caused pain. I thought this may be an appropriate time to discuss how much I disagreed with what he was teaching us.

I blurted out, "Jim, I disagree." To back up my case, I promptly quoted the scripture written by the Apostle Paul.

> "Brothers and sisters, I do not consider myself yet to have taken hold of it. But one thing I do: Forgetting what is behind and straining toward what is ahead; I press on toward the goal to win the prize for which God has called me heavenward in Christ Jesus."
> Philippians 3:13-14 NIV

As soon as I'd finished, I looked him in the eye. Our eyes deadlocked. Then, with a gentle smile, he told all of us to turn to Philippians chapter three. All eyes were on me. He asked me to begin at the very beginning of chapter three. Read it all the way through.

He asked me what Paul talked about in the verses before verse thirteen. I had to reread it. God opened my eyes. I saw that Paul did in fact rehash his life. He spoke of his confidence in the flesh. He spoke of how he was incredibly prideful of his upbringing. Paul spoke about where he came from and what he was taught. He even persecuted the church. I couldn't deny it. Paul did talk and boast about his past.

Jim looked around at everyone and said, "Unless we know what we have been healed, delivered and set free from, we don't have a testimony. What has Jesus done for you? How has He set you free and from what?"

My face turned red from humiliation, but I was relieved that I wasn't in some cult and hadn't made a huge mistake by coming here. I knew I had heard from God. Everything inside of me was confident about that. I was thankful that God still demonstrated His patience, love, and kindness by simply confirming His call like He had on that very special afternoon.

After all of that, we moved on to group, which was still very difficult for me. I was bound to my oath of never talk, never share my heart or thoughts, and never share my business. I learned that from a young age. My heart didn't know this kind of freedom. There was so much pain attached to so many things deep within my soul, how would I even begin to be stripped of shame?

The whole thing about putting my past behind and confessing sins had me confused. I hadn't learned these scriptures in this sense while in church. In my mind, these two scriptures were contradictory. What I had always understood was that we are not to dwell upon the things in our past. Those were all under the blood and were dealt with the day I accepted Jesus. But James 5:16 says we are to confess our sins one to another and pray for one another so that we may be healed.

Was God saying that I was permitted to express things that came up in my mind and heart? Throughout the past years, I had been told not to talk about them and to submit to God any of my thoughts that set themselves up against the Lord. *Was it really God bringing these things up so that I would have to deal with them and confess them?*

Was I supposed to speak up like the other women? Jim explained scripture upon scripture and showed me that unless I knew what I was delivered from, I wouldn't have a testimony. I honestly wanted to share my story. I always got so exhausted trying to restrain myself anytime anything about my past life came up. It always made me feel depressed, heavy, and fake.

One evening after quiet time, I had a conversation with one of the women in the program who shared some details about her past and what brought her to rehab. She shared how she lived like a queen running around with big time drug dealers and riding around in cars doing drugs while selling her body. She shared how she'd been part of a brothel and had perks because she'd always found herself with the main drug dealers that were in charge. Eventually it all came to an end because they were all busted by the police.

Her story was so similar to mine that I felt free to tell some of my story. I shared my experiences and didn't feel guilty or shameful. I didn't feel like I was breaking the rules of do not tell either. It was actually quite freeing not having to act fake. It felt incredible to tell the truth about who I used to be, what I used to do, and not feel the fear of being judged for it.

It felt so much like freedom. After that night, I believe I started to see a glimpse of what this whole Abba House thing was about. This may have been exactly what God was talking about when He told me to start sharing more of my testimony. It was starting with tearing down the lies, the fear, the shame, and the guilt. God was literally setting me free from me!

What a God who loves so much that He wants us free, not just born again, but free from the constant maddening thoughts that keep people in bondage. I went to bed that night feeling a sense of liberty and closed my eyes thinking how this just might be the beginning of being stripped of shame

.

Removing the Guilt

I was getting used to the daily routine, but I was still struggling with not having control over my medication. When I arrived at Abba House, I had to turn in my pain pills and ask the house mother for them when I needed them. She was instructed to give them as prescribed per the doctor's orders. I was prescribed one pill every four to six hours. Every morning I listened to the sarcastic voice in my head that told me how idiotic it was that I came here. *"Having to surrender my medication, didn't they know how much I needed them, my pain was real, didn't they know that?"* As I lay in bed I regretted the decision I made to come to Abba House. The thought of others knowing about and controlling my medication made me anxious. In addition to the voice in my head, there was a constant nagging feeling that urged me to leave the program, go home, and handle my own pain medication. Every morning I woke up irritated and anxious. My only motivation to get out of bed was to find the house mother and ask her for a pain pill.

It was around the third month when I realized that being around the women and always having someone by my side, whether I liked them or not, wasn't so terrible. It reminded me of the comfort I felt when I was a little girl and was always with my brother. I wasn't always alone because the program demanded accountability. Relationship was foundational and was genuinely helping me. I noticed that I wasn't so preoccupied with the pain and the desire for the pain pills. In fact, I was actually getting used to taking them as prescribed. Deep down I really did want off the pain pills. I had been on them since the day of the accident.

One day, a couple of Jim's friends came to visit: his mentor, Brother Don Van-Hoosier, and another guy named Scott. We prepared lunch as usual and they joined us. I thought the anxiety that I'd been feeling most of the morning was because of the guests. The idea of meeting these men who I don't know anything about really set me off. After we made our way into the living room and found our seats, my anxiety was out of control. It was so bad that I actually started shaking as if I had chills. This would have been one of those times where I would have popped a pill and waited to feel okay to be able to socialize, but here I didn't have that option.

Introductions went on for a few minutes. Meanwhile, in addition to the chills, my back started throbbing with intense pain. I adjusted my seating and squirmed around trying to get comfortable. I knew I needed to get a pain pill. I went on and on about my back, trying to manipulate my way into getting permission to get a hold of my house mother who was at the thrift store across the street. My intent was to say enough so that maybe they would see how badly I needed the medication. Perhaps they may even suggest contacting her and have her rush over to give me a pain pill. Instead, they offered to pray over me.

I stood up and everyone, including our guests, put their hands on me. As they did, the pain in my back intensified. After prayer, there was silence. Jim said he felt as though God had shown him that there was a deeper issue to this pain in my lower back. He went on to say that the chronic pain was a burden I had been carrying. He then asked, "What's chasing you?" I rambled on about the pressure of being in rehab while my parents are alone in another state. I explained I needed to be there with them so that I could take care of them. Then he asked me why I needed to take care of them. He asked if they were elderly. I explained they were in their early fifties and sixties. He asked if they were sick or disabled. I told him they were not. He was confused and asked me why I needed to take care of them. I told him that I felt like this was my responsibility as their daughter. I believed it was my job to take care of my parents no matter what. I was even mandated by my brother. Before he passed away, he told me that this was what I was supposed to do.

I was suddenly frightened at the thought of them being alone. I was a few hundred miles away from them and I started to feel the anger rise up. I still didn't know how to process emotion. I started to cry and confess my true feelings. I explained that the burden of this responsibility was overwhelming me. I felt like I had nothing planned for my life. I knew that I would be more than willing to be there for my folks one day, but at this point in time, they were perfectly able to care for themselves. I couldn't believe that I was actually telling people who I barely knew all of this. I began feeling guilty for having had those thoughts.

I stood there covered in guilt. I was so frustrated with myself. Then Jim shared what God showed him. He told me that I was carrying all that in my back. He said he believed I was carrying my father on one side of my back and my mother on the other side. He said there was an easier way to deal with this situation. He said I could trust God with my parents, which meant I had to quit doing his job and resign from the position of being their savior. He went on to suggest that I might even feel better if I trust God to take care of them. He asked me if I believed if God may be able to do a better job than I ever could. I had never heard this kind of talk before. The guilt really washed over me. I didn't want to feel like I was abandoning my folks, no matter what I had held in my heart towards them. We were still very much enmeshed in a blood is thicker than water kind of way.

I noticed the other two men praying. Brother Don had his head down, but his lips were moving. Even the ladies in the group were praying. My mind was racing. I was so used to being criticized for having feelings, but I felt a peace come over me that encouraged me.

Jim asked if I was ready to pray. "Father God, I repent for judging my mother for being helpless and not able to care for herself and for teaching me that my lot in life was to take care of her and my father. I repent for judging my father for inadvertently putting this responsibility on me to care for his wife and not telling me that I could be free from this. I repent for judging them for burdening me with the idea that I have to take care of them when they get older. I repent for judging my parents for putting this responsibility on me at such a young age. Forgive me Lord Jesus for not trusting you. I repent for being angry with my brother for also putting this on me. I confess I have been terribly afraid and very angry, not only at them, but also at You, Lord. I repent for believing the lies that I had to do all this and there would be no one to help me, including You, Lord. I repent for putting myself in Your place and thinking I had to control everything. I repent for thinking that I could do a much better job than You could and for not trusting in You to love them more than I ever could. I decided that if I didn't do this, no one would, not even you God. I have been putting this burden on myself. I renounce my controlling spirit. I renounce myself as ruler of my own universe and take myself off the throne. I stand down as their savior and ask you to take your rightful place in my life and in my heart. I give you my parents. In the name of Jesus I pray, Amen."

I waited in silence and within seconds, I felt God impress on me these words: "I will take care of my children. I love them more than you ever will, for they belong to me." I immediately began crying. Jim asked if the pain in my back was still present. The chronic pain had vanished, but I still felt discomfort when I bent over. Jim looked me in the eye and said, "Why don't you tell it to go?"

I had no clue what he was referring to. "Tell what to go?" I asked.

"The Spirit of pharmakeia," he said.

He explained that pharmakeia was the root word for pharmacy which also, per scripture, means witchcraft.

"You can tell it to go," he said "You are a child of God, aren't you? You have a legal right as a child of God to command this to go and make it leave."

I had no idea how to pray like this.

As I had already learned, I followed a guided prayer: "In the name of Jesus, I tell you to go! Spirit of pharmakeia, I don't need you anymore! You are not my friend, get out now, in Jesus' name!"

As soon as I finished that quick powerful prayer, I immediately felt a swoosh beginning from the tops of my feet up and across my body then up over my head. Imagine a large paint brush gently being brushed upward from the tops of your feet across your body and up over your head. That is what this felt like. I literally felt no pain in my body. I bent over and I moved my hips from side to side. There was no pain. It was really gone!

I looked around and everyone was staring at me in amazement. I excused myself to the restroom because I wanted to splash some water on my face. When I came out of the bathroom, everyone was smiling. They said I looked different. It was that same difference I saw when someone received healing in group.

I finished out the group with prayers of asking God to forgive me for being such a rebellious daughter to my parents. It was as if God could finally show me that I too responded in ugly ways to my parents, even before all those terrible things happened to me. God was able to show me that there were things that I did to hurt my parents. In front of all these witnesses, I confessed my hardened heart, my bitterness, and my rebellion. I asked God to wash me clean and if there were any more things hidden in my heart, expose them and cleanse me. I desperately wanted my family to be happy. It had been something I wanted since I was a young girl. It was always in my heart and it still was as an adult. I cried and cried. Jesus took that afternoon to take my burden, deliver me from a demonic spirit, and wash me clean of guilt.

No one said a word. They sat and listened as Jesus and I were in the middle of that amazing miracle. I felt peace. This peace was a peace that takes up residence inside of you; it has life, it has breath, and it consumes your entire being.

I noticed I wasn't the only one crying. I never knew God did things like this. I never believed others would sit and cry and pray with me like the girls who were in that group did that afternoon. I felt awkward because all eyes were on me. Everyone was smiling and that comforted my heart. I noticed that the guilt I had been carrying for so long was also gone. I felt so much lighter and I knew everything was going to be okay. Finally, I asked if I could do one more thing. I asked if I could flush the remaining pain pills I had down the toilet. In no time, my house mother was contacted. When she showed up, the med box was immediately opened. She handed me the prescription bottle containing the very things I considered my savior. We walked to the bathroom and I lifted the toilet seat and opened the bottle. Without even thinking another thought, I dumped them into the toilet.

I flushed those pills and that spirit of pharmakeia, that spirit of witchcraft right, down the toilet. Down into the sewage they went. We threw that stinking bottle in the trash. God stripped me from a burden I couldn't carry. The demonic spirit, guilt, six years of doctors, pain, pain pills, and an addiction to narcotics were finally gone!

Recovery had officially started and I was on a new path. I was officially chemical free. God's grace was real and He was all over me. He was healing me, delivering me, and loving me. There was no way that I would have flushed those pills down the toilet without panicking on my own. The pain did try to come back and I did experience the awkwardness of detox. I felt out of sorts in more ways than one. I could literally feel the stuff coming out of my system. In fact, the very next day that muscle aches and spasms in my legs and lower back returned. With them came massive anxiety and fierce irritability. I knew in my heart that a miracle had taken place because through it all, the desire for those pills did not return. God had truly taken the desire to be medicated completely away and that's how I knew without a shadow of doubt that something genuine had taken place.

I believe that when I decided not to budge, that's when all the nagging soreness, cramping, and pain finally diminished all together. I had been under doctors' care and medication for so long that I had forgotten what it was like to be free from the burdens of sickness, pain, and infirmity. I would no longer have to go to the doctors every thirty days and waste a whole day sitting in waiting rooms, doctor's offices, and pharmacies. Now that I didn't have the pain pills that hid my true feelings and gave me a boost of confidence when I needed it, the terror really set in.

I had a dream one night that seemed so real. In this dream, I saw a younger version of myself. I was in a bedroom with the door slightly cracked open. I was peeking out. That was it. That was the entire dream. I shared it with the director's wife and she asked me if I was ready to come out and play. Her response caught me off guard. *What did that mean?* I was still so afraid to talk about anything substantial, especially the sexual abuse I endured. *How would God heal my broken heart and shattered spirit? I knew he could heal bodies and deliver the demon called pharmakeia, but could he heal a vulnerable heart? Wasn't it my vulnerability that always led to me being hurt?*

I was terrified to come out from under this fear and share this part of my life. I had always felt unsafe, especially around people I didn't really know. I didn't care if these people professed Jesus. I believed that no matter how much we love Jesus and want to walk out a clean spirit led life, people are people and they can be selfish and carnal and hurt you even though they say they love Jesus. I didn't have problems taking things to God in prayer, but when it came to group, my insides shook from fright. To me, this was nothing like dealing with the parent and pharmakeia thing. This was way too intrusive.

Chris showed up for group the following week and asked me if I was ready to come out and play? With a sincere smile, she then asked how I was doing. Anxiety immediately gripped me and I felt a tug inside. The Holy Spirit began to work through her.

Before I knew it, images of the car accident flashed in my mind. As we began tracing that anxious emotion backwards, we discovered where those feelings of fear first emerged.

My mind went back to my brother's friend. I was being vulnerable and trusting when I allowed him to come inside and wait. I paid dearly for trusting him. He took advantage of my innocence and created the fear. The next image was of my cousin. He had taken advantage of me inside my home where I was supposed to be safe. Not only had I been deceived, but my parents were also deceived by them. The fear was caused because I had already experienced abuse with the neighbor. Then I remembered overhearing my father blaming me for my abuse. I started feeling like I was losing my mind. I felt outside of myself, thinking that I might have to go to the mental hospital. I felt like we opened up something that should have been left alone. Images of being blind folded and taken raced through my mind as I violently scribbled on my pad with a ballpoint pen. My eyes closed tightly and I was completely outside of myself.

The Prayer Minister asked, "What do you see? What's going on?"

I said, "I feel so scared. I feel like I am losing my mind. I want my brother!" I was crying hysterically. "It's dark in here." A small voice uttered from deep within.

The Prayer Minister said. "Ask Jesus to come and get you."

"Jesus, would you come and get me?" I cried.

I started to hyperventilate. I felt like I would black out. The rage brewed inside of me and I felt the spirit of murder fill my heart. I let out such a scream that startled even me. The pain came rushing out like a flood. I screamed, I cussed, and I said things that I've always wanted to say, but never was permitted to say. All that fear that had been tied to all those times when I was forced to keep quiet: The blame I carried in my heart towards myself and towards everyone else I believed was completely at fault. It all came rushing out. Finally, the tears came like a torrential rain through my eyes. The pain was being washed away; God was making a way in the desert and rivers in the desert. God was doing a new thing in my life. With my eyes still closed, I saw my brother reaching out for me. I was trapped in a dark dungeon covered by a locked medieval castle door. I saw his hand and I reached out for it. In that immediate moment, my brother's face turned to Jesus' face and what was my brother's hand was now Jesus' hand. It was Jess who pulled me out of the dungeon of darkness, just like the man who gently lifted me out of my truck the day of that devastating accident that nearly took my life. Jesus Himself showed up. He came and got me. Through the torrents of tears, Jesus washed away years of torment, fear, blame and pain.

After this miraculous moment took place, several people in the room said they had images of Jesus in their mind. They too had experienced a miraculous spiritual encounter where Jesus allowed Himself to be seen in many forms and many ways that afternoon. Everyone silently watched as I caught my breath while sitting in the presence of Jesus.

I shared with the group something that I had never shared with anyone. I had been blind folded and taken by three men. I was brutally violated. I was terrified. It was painful and I needed it to stop. I wanted to go home and I couldn't get free. I was overpowered and couldn't make it stop. I didn't know where I was because I was blind folded. I was terrified. I needed my brother to come save me, but he was dead. I disassociated to protect myself and hid deep down inside as I did when it first began as a young girl.

They asked if I was ready to forgive my perpetrators and I gladly said yes. "Lord Jesus, I choose to forgive my neighbor for taking advantage of me. I forgive him for stealing my innocence and creeping around my house keeping me in fear and isolated. I forgive him for lying to me, for stealing my voice, for making me feel so afraid, and for causing me to hide in fear. Lord, I forgive my father for not giving me a chance to talk that night, for not comforting me in my time of need, for not giving me a chance to give my side of the story. I forgive him for making me feel as though I did something to him and against his name. I forgive my dad for not defending me and not coming to my aid emotionally. I forgive him for blaming me and allowing fear to take over my life. I forgive him for making me feel rejected and not valuable enough to protect, nurture, and love. Lord, what do you want to show me? What's the truth about me, Jesus?"

I knew that Jesus was right there with me. I heard a still small voice say, "You are safe to come out because I have always wanted you, for I created you. You are perfect in my sight. I have made you whiter than snow, you are free to speak, and you will no longer walk in fear, for I am your Father and I have called you by name. I love you!"

Stripped of Shame

That little girl who was hiding in her room and chained in a dungeon, was released from her prison of fear by Jesus. Those feelings and emotions of fear were gone. I wasn't afraid to talk. That pressure and fear was completely gone. I could feel a real tangible difference inside myself. I am referring to my inner man the Bible talks about. Some said I even looked brighter, my face was glowing. Not only that, they said my voice changed and I sounded different. It was then that I realized that the unfamiliar voice that had uttered out to God for help after the accident was this voice. The voice of a terrified, wounded and broken young girl who had been stuck in darkness and who had not had a chance to live. She desperately wanted a chance at life and Jesus heard her cry. All these years trapped in a dungeon of pain, fear, rejection and darkness.

What a powerful revelation from such a powerful God! After all these years it was God and only God who lifted off and freed me from the guilt and not only that but also removed the core of my fear. How could I possibly doubt the power of salvation after this? What could I fight? I had no resistance. I was ready to allow God to go even deeper into my soul, continuing this sanctification that was literally transforming me from the inside out. Jesus was cleansing me of all unrighteousness which brought healing to my soul and filling me with great peace. Jesus was loving me to a new life in Him.

I have always wondered how Jesus had so much peace. How could He go about doing good and healing all those who were oppressed all the while being constantly followed around by people who wanted to crucify Him? *How could Jesus not be offended?*

151

Doreen Stumpf

How did the critical, mocking words of the Pharisees, Sadducees, and priests not have an effect on Him? How did the devil not succeed at stealing Jesus' peace?

Then I understood something. Jesus didn't have any sin! It is sin that gives the enemy a foothold or place (ground) or an opportunity. The ability of demons to harass Christians is based on the degree to which we walk in the Light. Jesus is the Light! He is the Light of the world, so since Jesus was sinless, the devil and his minions had no power over Jesus, therefore He could walk in peace because there wasn't any ground given to the enemy. Jesus didn't have bitterness or hatred in His heart. He didn't judge others unrighteous. He certainly didn't dishonor His parent's or make any rash vows. He didn't involve Himself in fornication, bribery, witchcraft or bowed down to idols. He most certainly didn't lie. He told the truth! Jesus is the truth! So the enemy was rendered powerless in this respect. Jesus Himself is peace. He was able to be at peace because there was no darkness in Him. The devil didn't have any ground.

I realized that each time I dealt with these ungodly truths confessing them and bringing them into the light God was helping me get back more ground, the ground of my heart that is. As I confessed not only the sin, but all my hatred, judgments, vows and ungodly beliefs, He was setting me free and removing the power of those sins that kept me in bondage. God was literally breaking the devil's power in my life by taking back any ground that had been given to him when I sinned. This is what true forgiveness looks like and feels like!

Removing the Shame

As my graduation date grew near, healings were happening daily. I remember being so exhausted from all the emotional healing. God is faithful. He didn't stop exposing the lies my heart held. In fact, I remembered hearing once that approximately eighty percent of illnesses may be psychosomatic. I'm not saying that my sickness was only in my head, but I do believe that some of the other causes could've simply been emotionally related. In each passing day I kept myself wide open trusting Jesus in this process as He continued to show me additional fears, attitudes, beliefs, and even a few harassing spirits still intent on keeping me in bondage. I was gaining more and more ground by the day.

One day while praying, I suddenly felt a stirring. It was an uncomfortable agitation rumbling around deep inside me. Not really knowing what it was, I immediately did what I had been learning to do: I prayed. Then I paused and waited. Nothing came immediately to mind. Instead of jumping to conclusions or worse, I meditated. While I sat waiting on God, Chris pulled up to the house. She was in a hurry and explained she was only there to drop off a piece of carpet. After laying it down in the living room she headed back toward the sliding glass doors and waved goodbye. As soon as she disappeared out of sight, I knew I had to run out and catch her and ask her to pray with me. I jumped to my feet, ran outside, and caught her just in time. I asked if she had a minute to pray with me. She said yes.

"What's up girl?" Chris asked.

"Not sure," I replied. "I'm just feeling a stirring inside, I have no idea what's going on inside of me; I just don't feel at peace. I've been praying and I'm not getting anything."

"So, what are you feeling?" she asked.

"Frustration and confusion," I answered.

"In the name of Jesus, confusion go. Confusion is from the devil and has no place here," she said. "Go now! So what are you feeling now?"

"Anger," I replied.

"What are you angry about?" she asked.

I screamed out, "My life!"

Before I knew what was going on, she was on her knees in front of me and she looked into my eyes. She seemed to be following something going from one side of my face to the other. She was following my eyes and I was trembling. I could feel something going from one eyeball to the other and back. I watched her as she followed along with her eyes.

She yelled, "You foul spirit, in the name of Jesus go! Get out now! In Jesus' name, you foul spirit, you must leave!"

Stripped of Shame

When she had finished saying the last sentence, my right leg started kicking up and down. I grabbed hold of her shoulders with my hands and violently shook her. I was screaming. I had no idea what I was doing or what was happening. This scream just came wailing out of me. When it was over, I fell back into the chair and exhaled this huge breath. I don't have words to explain the intensity of what I felt and what had happened. I hadn't been too acquainted with deliverance nor did I claim to understand this stuff, but one thing was certain something vacated my body.

After she left, I sat there on that couch pondering and praying, asking God for understanding. *Lord, what just happened? What was that?*

I sat waiting on the Lord. A sense of safety and assurance came over me, immediately followed by a tsunami of memories. I remembered how much I had hated my name. I remembered how much I hated being me. God was showing me all the horrible, detestable things I had said and done to myself. I thought of the accident and how I couldn't bare exposing who I really was. For as long as I had remembered, I desperately ran from my true identity. I had so many names, especially after running away from home. At some point I finally accepted just being Dede. I rejected the name I was born with. In my mind, I didn't really have a name or an identity other than shame.

Shame held my destiny and any hope that I may have had for the future. Shame was the core of my being. Shame told me who I was. It defined my character and my personality. It told me what I could expect from myself. I was wrapped up in grave

155

clothes of ungodly beliefs that something was terribly wrong with me. Shame caused me to believe that I was uniquely and hopelessly flawed. Every mistake I made said I was a mistake. I strongly believed that I was not good enough, not valuable or important. I believed that I was a flat out defect created for rejection. Shame was my identity. It was the very thing that kept me striving, angry, confused, and jealous. Shame kept me bound in depression because I believed I could never measure up. Shame fueled the self-hatred I held onto which ultimately kept me in the cycle of wishing death upon myself.

Shame kept me in bondage to the spirit of control which I operated in order to keep back who I believed I was. Shame filled my life with so much fear. Much like Eve in Genesis chapter three. Eve was tempted by satan and chose to eat the fruit of the tree of the knowledge of good and evil. The Bible said when she did that, well when she and Adam did that, their eyes were opened and they knew they were naked. See I knew something was wrong with me, in a sense I knew I was naked and I didn't want anyone to see me so I hid. I hid within myself not wanting to expose the real me. Shame consumed me and was that constant whisper in my ear much like how the snake whispered in Eve's ear in the garden, but he didn't tell me I'd be like God, it told me I was a failure and no one could nor would ever love a bad girl like me.

In that moment, God opened up my eyes and permitted me to see a picture of my life. I saw seeds. These seeds were seeds that were planted in me, my garden, my heart, and throughout all these years, these seeds that were planted grew. He showed me how I had spent a lifetime cursing myself, putting myself down, turning on myself, and allowing people to hurt me. He showed me how I agreed with other people who spoke negatively to me and spoke negative words over me. Finally, God showed me the day I set myself up against myself when I chose to hate myself and call myself by other names. When I rejected myself, I became divided. It was in that fragmented state that I became open game and subject to desolation according to the Bible. But Jesus knew their thoughts and said to them: "Every kingdom divided against itself is brought to desolation, and every city or house divided against itself will not stand" Matthew 12:25.

God showed me how these shame based inner beliefs which I called my truths, were planted throughout my childhood. Those shame based seeds grew firm in my adolescence and now I had reaped the fruit of them as an adult. They were so deceptive and were only designed to destroy me. It was this shame based belief that led me to the place where I decided I couldn't take it anymore and would take my own life. I didn't know of any other way. I didn't know how to get free from all that pain.

God in His amazing grace was gently freeing me of a lifetime of being so ashamed of who I was. He gently unraveled the grave clothes I had wrapped myself in similar to Adam and Eve. They too made clothes to cover themselves because they went from a mindset that they were naked and unashamed to realizing they were naked and that something was terribly wrong with them. I jumped on the opportunity to work alongside God by emptying myself of years and years of self-imposed curses by doing exactly what 1 John 1:9 says to do. I started confessing all the horrible things I had spoken over myself. I confessed to hating myself. I confessed to calling myself ugly, fat, and hopeless. I confessed to blaming myself for all that had been done to me. I confessed to agreeing with the devil on all those negative thoughts I had had about myself. I confessed to rejecting myself and dividing myself up. I confessed to betraying my own conscience and allowing immorality to defile my body and inner man. I made a list of everyone I could remember I had illicit affairs with, even people I became emotionally tied to and one by one broke soul ties with each one of them. I broke the power of any negative words that were spoken over me, to me and about me from people who were in authority. I even broke the power of ungodly agreements I made with people. I continued confessing judgments I remembered I made about myself. So many times I sat in front of a mirror and criticized myself, spoke hateful things to myself and rejected my appearance, intellect and weight. I loosened myself from any unrealistic standards I had bound myself to. With each confession came the realization of how much I really was my own worst enemy. Soon I started to feel the fogginess of the facades disappearing.

But then something profound happened. I literally saw myself as a dirty dust rag. I cannot possibly put into words the reality of this revelation. I literally could see and feel and I knew without a doubt, in comparison to God, that I was a dirty dust rag.–Without any hesitation I confessed my selfish pride. In that second, I surrendered from my innermost being and gave up. It was the combination of shame and the pride of life that compelled me to continually fight to prove not only to my parents and others around me, but mainly to myself, that I can do anything I wanted. I had put myself first and when I decided to put myself first unknowingly, I had also erected myself up as an idol. I had actually worshipped myself and wanted all things to myself: the men, the money, the drugs, the ruthless undertakings, and all the pain I caused others. It was all in the name of Doreen.

Through the torrent of tears, I continued to acknowledge my sins and confess. God was going deeper. It became quite clear that what I had blamed everyone else for doing, I too had done. I hurt others just as I had been hurt. Hurting people hurt people. I had taken my own pain out on everyone around me and, as a result, I continued the cycle of abuse, drugs, alcoholism, pain, bitterness, unforgiveness, entanglements, enmeshment, idol worshiping, lust, gambling, the love of money, and fornication.

It felt like a mighty rushing wind had filled my human temple and its effects were making room for a new root system. The bitter roots that had been formed in me since my childhood were being uprooted and replaced with the truth of who I am in Christ. The Holy Spirit was healing and comforting me as God was developing in me a consecration of true righteousness and holiness. Jesus Himself was removing the shame and giving me an identity.

I sat there caught up in bliss with the Holy Spirit of God. Wave after wave of His love washed over me. I could feel the peace that surpasses all understanding saturating my heart. I couldn't help but pray, "Lord, I repent for hating myself so much. I repent for despising myself so much that I wanted to take my own life. I repent for calling unclean what you call clean. For you word says, what God calls clean, don't call it unclean. Acts 10:15. I repent for believing all those lies about me, whom you yourself chose to fill with your spirit. I repent for being so prideful and only caring about what man thinks about me instead of being concerned about what you may think about me. I renounce idolatry which is non-other than seeking out the approval of man. I am so sorry Lord that I ignored you and focused only on me. Lord help me be me and Lord, forgive me I was wrong about all this."

I waited silently for the voice of God to speak, and then as clear as day the voice that brought me closer to my heavenly Father spoke in my heart saying, "Doreen, you are my beloved daughter. I love you with all my heart I am proud of you and am very happy to call you mine. I will never leave you, nor forsake you, for you are mine and I chose you. No one can take you out of my hands for I delicately made and designed you to be fashioned after my Son, whom I dearly love. He sacrificed for you and you will reap the blessing of his suffering. I love you my daughter, Doreen."

God called me by my name Doreen. When I looked up my name or I should say I Googled it, the name Doreen is of Hebrew origin and means "Gift of God"! If anyone knows how to make you feel so special it is our heavenly Father. From that day forward, Dede was replaced with Doreen. For the first time in what was a lifetime for me, I didn't feel anything negative towards that name. I actually felt a sense of joy and looked forward to being reintroduced to her and finding out who she was. God had delivered me from a murderous spirit that afternoon, a spirit that only came to kill me, steal my identity, and destroy my future. But God handed me back my identity and my name. I willingly accepted. God stripped me of shame!

Redemption at the Foot of the Cross

One month away from graduation, the ministry geared up for their yearly trip to Epworth by the Sea, a three day conference where people from all over get together to worship, pray, hangout, get baptized, have tons of fun, and eat.

We arrived safely one Friday afternoon and hurriedly settled in our rooms. We were all looking forward to—the buffet. There was always such good food and coffee! The atmosphere sizzled with love as everyone greeted one another with a lot of hugs and big smiles. Once dinner was finished, everyone made their way to our first meeting and worship service. After introductions, we reviewed the weekend itinerary. The worship team made their way to the stage. There were people of all ages and the anticipation of experiencing the tangible presence of God was at an all time high.

Doreen Stumpf

The worship leader stepped up to the microphone to welcome everyone and open in prayer. The lights were dimmed and the worship began. I closed my eyes and whispered a little prayer asking God if it was possible to go even deeper, then I wanted to go where He wanted to go. I lifted my hands and began to worship from the depth of my soul. The night ended after a couple of hours and everyone headed back to their rooms for a good night sleep. We were excited about what Saturday would bring.

No alarms were needed the next morning as the excitement in the air was our alarm clock. The sun was shining bright and you could feel the joy and expectations of a glorious day ahead. After breakfast at the buffet, everyone met back up at the hall where we had morning worship and heard the word of God. After lunch, those headed to the beach for baptisms boarded a bus. The rest stayed back for a break at the pools or returned to the hall for private prayer or prophecy. I headed to the beach to participate in the water baptisms.

Once we gathered on the beach, I saw people of all ages make their way into the water and ready themselves to be baptized. What a sight! Looking out onto those standing in that cold water reaching out to God, trusting Him to save their souls, confirms that there are people who believe that this earth is not our final destination. There was so much more and all of us gathered there that day were surely a definite outward sign. Joy of new life splashed everywhere. People who were not with our party came into the water and asked to be baptized. I had never been to anything like this before. God was showing me that

164

we were witnessing to the people on the beach. It reminded me of the day I was on the beach looking out into the ocean blue wanting to die, but now I was in the ocean blue living. What started out as a death wish just seven years before, ended in life on the beach. I was lit up with life as we boarded the bus to head back.

I felt like for the first time in my life I could see. I could see how the world and all its lustful pleasures can offer people a false sense of security and distort their identity. I could see how the world sucks them in and they get lost in it. I could see how the deception of money, power, and a good life controls people. I could see that the hunger for more and having to prove to themselves and others can be a burden and be very damaging to relationships. As the bus slowed down to turn, I happened to catch a young man gassing up his pickup truck. As the bus idled in that turn, the young man and I caught each other's eyes. I flashed back to the time that I was lost on the interstate trying to find Georgia 400 and stopped for directions. I remembered that guy who was gassing up his pick up and who asked me if I was lost and needed directions. It was this guy who pointed me in the right direction. As we made the final turn, he smiled at me. I just stared until he and the gas station were out of sight.

My heart was like fire burning within me blowing up with sheer excitement. *Was that the same guy from the gas station? Was it Jesus? Or was he an angel of God showing up again to confirm that I was in the perfect will of God? Who were these random men who showed up from time to time pulling me out of upside down trucks and pointing me in the right direction when I got lost?*

We returned to our rooms and prepared for dinner and another night of praise and worship. When we got to the hall, the lights were already dimmed. The worship team had already started. People were praying in their heavenly language and the atmosphere was primed and ready. The Spirit of God was strong in that place. The girls and I found our seats and immediately started singing along with the music. I looked up front and saw the director of Abba House and his wife standing with their hands raised. They were praising God along with mostly everyone in the room. I closed my eyes and found that place in my spirit where I touch Jesus. But then, seemingly out of nowhere, I heard a still small voice in my ear that said, "You hate me." I knew this was an attack from the devil. I started to feel uneasy.

My spirit was restless. My euphoria was slowly vanishing and I heard the voice again. Visions bubbled out of my heart and I remembered storming into the church, ripping my necklace with the cross of Jesus on it off my neck, throwing it on the floor of the altar, spitting on it, and then spinning around on my heel as I headed towards the front doors to leave. Then I saw how I spun back around one more time sticking out my middle finger and defiling the house of God by telling God to go to hell.

The Holy Spirit of God was confronting me. He was showing me all those offenses, anger, and rage I held in my heart all these years. The anger and rage were not entirely directed toward my parents, myself, or even the people who abused me. They were directed towards Him. I stood frozen when all of a sudden my ears picked up the sounds of the worship and noticed the worship leader on stage singing one lyric of a song over and over again. It was slightly irritating. I hadn't experienced worship like that before. It was prophetic worship, which I had not been exposed to before.

I looked over to my Abba sister standing next to me and asked her if she would walk to the ladies room with me. As we walked, we talked about the repetition of the music. We giggled a bit and made our way into the ladies room. When we came out of the stalls, we were laughing hysterically. We were acting like two drunken women as we nearly fell over the sinks washing our hands. My friend looked at me and asked what was going on with us, but we couldn't make heads or tails of it. We kept laughing and laughing. I remembered seeing this before where people are hit with the spirit of God and enjoy a time of bliss and laughter. It's called being drunk in the spirit.

After a few more moments of uncontrollable laughter, we washed our hands and headed back out. To my surprise, that same song was still going on! I sat down in my seat and put my head down. Suddenly something changed in me. I became quite somber and felt a nudge in my spirit. I started to sense I needed to go up to the altar. I waited a few more minutes, but it wouldn't go away. I finally gave in to the nudging, got up out of the chair, and made my way to the altar.

As I was walking down the aisle, I glanced around at everyone. There were many people at the altar who were on their knees praying. Some were crying and others prayed in their heavenly language. I looked up and gazed at the cross. Those memories flashed across my mind again of when I went into that church. I felt like my chest was going to burst. I

167

began to weep. I desperately wanted my dad, my earthly father. I needed him! I wanted to be with him. This feeling now sabotaging any joy I had, overwhelmed me. It took my breath away. Feelings of abandonment gripped my heart. My heart ached for my earthly father to have some part in and of my life. I desperately wanted to be held in his arms as he did when I was just a toddler. It was there where I felt safe, loved and accepted. The weeping turned into sobbing and then into a convulsive cry.

The instruments played and the worship went on. I began to confess to God my feelings about all the things that I believe He did to me. Through the frustration, anger, hurt, and downpour of tears I uttered, "I hate you for letting these things happen to me. What kind of God does this to people? I blame you God. I blame you! I feel like you allowed me to be born only to have me suffer, be rejected, and be beaten all the while you sit in heaven and watched. You did nothing! Why did you allow my brother to die? Why did you allow my family to fall apart? Why didn't you stop my family from fighting so much? Why did you allow all those people to hurt me? Why weren't you there to protect me?"

I was at the foot of the cross convulsing in tears. I must have been down there for quite some time when I felt someone grab my arms and lift me up. My body was limp and heavy with exhaustion. God was doing something. Jim picked me up and held me as the Spirit of God continued cleansing me and set things right in my heart. The flood gates had opened deep within me. I cried and wailed. I couldn't stop. God was taking all the pain, disappointment, and anger away from me. I felt someone behind me wrapping their arms around me. It was Jim's wife, Chris. They both had their arms wrapped around me, cocooning me in their arms as God was healing my heart.

Chris turned me around and made me look into her eyes and assured me that I would be alright. Those were the same words I heard right after the accident while sitting in my old room by myself. My spirit felt like a tornado had passed through it. As the convulsions slowly ceased I could see in my spirit that there is a throne that sits in the center of my heart. I believe it is called the mercy seat. In that seat sat my earthly father. I idolized him. I desperately needed his love and attention that I had put him above everyone including God. I was hurt by so many men and the one man I loved the most and needed to tell me who I was and why I existed, who alone was my night and shining armor, who I needed to protect me from the bad men didn't give me any of that. He took care of me, provided for me and I never went without, except the one thing I needed the most: him.

God knew this. God knew that on the day that I stormed into that church I was so hurt, not only because of my brother's death but because. I needed my dad! So, that day God answered my prayer. We went deeper and we went where God wanted to go. God removed my father from this throne in my heart and exchanged places with him. God took His rightful place and took from me a lifetime of toiling to be heard, seen and valued.

I stood at the foot of the cross that night and officially gave up. I fully surrendered whatever I might have left in me. I looked at the cross and humbly said, "Lord Jesus, God Almighty, I am sorry!

169

Doreen Stumpf

Would You forgive me for agreeing with the devil and siding with him? Would You forgive me, Lord Jesus, for going into your house of worship and defiling it the way I did? I'm asking for mercy and your forgiveness for my blatant disobedience and straight-out-defiant attitude toward You and Your house. I was wrong for blaming you, Lord God, I was so wrong."

My heart emptied the burden of guilt and condemnation as God redeemed me that day at the foot of the cross. That deep burden of sin was once and for all completely removed from my heart. Once again, faithful God cleansed me of unrighteousness. I broke with true sorrowful repentance of my behavior and attitude toward God, the Creator of all life! What God did that day changed me forever. He traded places in my heart with my dad so that I could be free from the bondage of man. Only God can give that absolute pure love. His agape love is life-giving and undefiled.

That weekend ended beautifully. The next few weeks blew by and I finished the program. The day I walked on stage to receive my certificate, I remembered the day I set off on this wild adventure. If someone would have told me what this was going to look like, I know I would have never left Florida. The things I have told you and described to you on paper, doesn't come close to the real experiential moments of the manifested presence of God.

When God shows up whatever is not of Him must leave and anything that is above Him must be brought low. He will not share His glory and nor will He allow anyone to take what in His. He is a jealous God. His love is fierce. His love is powerful. His love

170

is gentle and kind and so comforting. He always knows exactly what we need and when we need it. Most importantly He loves with a fierce love and He is so desperate to share it with His creation.

God is constantly wooing His creation to come to Him just so He can saturate us with His love. Who wouldn't want to experience love? The shame, fear, and guilt that plagued my life and stole from me are gone. Do I deal with things still? Sure do. The key is knowing what to do with it when it shows up knocking wanting reentry. I love Jesus with all my heart, soul and mind. I couldn't do that if He didn't first love me.

What God did for me, every attempt of man could not. It was God who stripped me of shame. My prayer for you today is that you will come to know God, your true Father, the way I have. His love for you is so strong that He sent His only Son to die for you! He wants to give you a hope and a future and to remind you that you too have an unforgettable story and that unforgettable story is you.

A Prayer of Salvation

Lord I come to you today broken and wounded
and lost. I ask you to get me started on the road to
recovery and strip me of shame. I invite you into my
heart as my Lord and Savior. Lord I may not
Know a whole lot about you, but whatever you
have I want!
Amen!

A Prayer for Healing the Wounded Spirit

Father you are so wonderful and so protective of
me; I cry out to you to come and heal my wounded
spirit. Thank you for your loving presence. I use now
the blood of Jesus to cleanse my mind, my thinking,
and my memories. Please bring your cleansing
presence into what I think, I believe and what I have

Doreen Stumpf

stored in my memories. Let the blood of Jesus flow over my ears, and my mouth; let it pour over each of the gates where destruction has entered in – through what I have heard, seen or spoken.

I lose the cleansing blood upon my heart and my emotions, representing the core of my being. I also declare that your cleansing blood, go deep into the hidden wounds of my inner man, deep into the secret wounds, and deeper still into the old dark wounds. Lord release the oil of the Holy Spirit. Bring your healing presence upon my mind, my thinking, my beliefs, and my memories.

Heal my faulty thinking and the lies behind this thinking. Heal the pain stored in these memories. Please release the oil of healing into my heart and my emotions; into all the broken places.

Holy Spirit, bring your healing presence into the deep places of my inner man, into the old wounds, the hidden wounds and into the dark secret wounds.

Father, please wrap me in your presence, cocoon me in your love. Will you watch over me and guard me in this season of healing. I speak your Word of truth and affirmation into my soul – renewing my mind. I release myself completely into your care knowing that you are faithful to heal, restore, and to renew. I declare, your Kingdom come and your will be done!

In the mighty name of Jesus, I pray
Amen!

A Prayer for a Heart of Flesh

Lord, I have developed a defense to keep myself
from being seen. I have built a hiding place to protect
myself from hurt. I know that this "protection"
blocks the love, warmth and nurture for which I long.
I come to You, Lord, because I am helpless to
change. I invite You into my life to take down the
wall. I want You to be my defense. Lord, help me to
become vulnerable, to risk love. Bring to death my
heart of stone and give me a heart of flesh. In Jesus
Name I pray. Amen.

Forgiveness Prayer

Lord, I know that you are not like anyone who
has ever hurt me. I know that you are not like me. I
don't know how to make forgiveness happen. I can't
cleanse my heart or change my feelings. I don't know
how to trust, and I'm afraid to hold my heart open.
But today I'm making a choice to forgive. I know I'll
have to choose again and again until You make
forgiveness real and complete in me. God, give me
the willingness and strength to persevere in choosing
until forgiveness is accomplished in me by Your love.
I choose to forgive my father for..........
I choose to forgive my mother for ....
Forgive ~~in~~ me all my sinful responses .....
Father, I let go of all resentments and bitterness
stored in my heart. Wash me clean and sanctify me.
Forgive me for all condemning judgments I have
made. Give me a new and right spirit within me that

Doreen Stumpf

will enable me to hate sin but look with Your
compassion and love upon the sinner.
Heal the wounded heart of the child within me.
Pour your love in. Bless those who wounded me.
Forgive me, Lord for projecting my childish pictures
in relation to parents onto You, and onto others,
especially those I love. Bring those pictures to death.
Let Your light shine, into all the hidden places of my
heart. Enlighten the eyes of my heart, Lord to see
You and love you as You really are and to walk in
Your way.
In Jesus Name.
Amen.

Acknowledgments

This book is a tribute to Jesus! He is the rock I stand on. He is my story, He is my song! It is Jesus I thank in every aspect and in every breath I take. For without my King, I would be dead!

Next, I thank my best friend and husband, Robert. The work done to I don't think I would have completed this book would it not have been without his prayers and support. He is my champion. He has been with me at every turn. When I came up against obstacles, whether they were spiritual or physical, my husband was my support, my friend, and my mainstay. He is immovable when it comes to Jesus and standing on the promises of God. That is exactly what I needed! Having this valiant warrior of Christ praying and standing beside me at all times is why this project was completed. Your daily devotion to our Lord and Savior sustained me and gave me hope through this undertaking. You have been such a supreme example of Christ's love and forgiveness.

Through your patient endurance and steadfast love, you have proven to me that Jesus does live in the heart of man. It is by your example as a husband to his wife that I have become stronger. Because of your constant pursuit for the One who gives us Life, we together have grown and become one as it was always meant to be. I love you!

I am grateful to all those who have inspired me and those who cheered me on. Thank you to everyone who walked with me through the times I wanted to quit and those who have hung in there and prayed and interceded for me.

I especially want to thank Teila Tankersley, Darin Carrol, and Marvie Kothman. It was Teila who was my muse. She inspired me to write my story. I give my utmost gratitude to Teila and her family. Thank you for seeing what God would do with my story. Others have encouraged me in the same way and I thank each and every one of you!

Nobody has been more precious to me through all of this than my family: my precious father, mother, and son. My parents, despite it all, never gave up on me. Their sheer determination to make it in this life and provide what they could to the best of their ability is more than I could have ever asked for. I may have not been as grateful back then as I am today, but my heart knows it always has a home with Dad and Mom! I love you into eternity!

To my son. I am so blessed to have you as my son. Through it all, you pushed through. You were determined, forgiving, and compassionate. You have more wisdom than any other person I know of your age. You are my inspiration, my love, and I am so proud of you!

Finally, to Jim and Chris Sharp, two people who committed themselves to the call of God on their lives. There are not enough words to say in thanks to the both of you and your family, I hope this book says it all! Out of your obedience came Abba House, Inc., a Christ-centered residential recovery treatment center for women and their children. It is because of the freedom God revealed to me through that ministry that I gained the courage to write *Stripped of Shame*. Thank you, Jim & Chris! (For more information on Abba House, visit www.abbahousemiddlega.com)

A special thanks to Pastors Mike and Donna DeBehnke, Haas and Debbie Mengoli, Darrin Carrol, Gloria Carrol, the Tankersley Family, and Pastors Trey and Shannon Dickerson.

Finally, I praise God for John and Cheryl Bullock. I first met them as members of a *Being Made Whole* group that Robert and I were hosting when we were in Colorado. It turned out to be a divine connection. John, author of "Seeing with Fresh Eyes," has been willing to freely edit anything I threw at him with a servant's heart. His willingness to help me complete this book and shoulder me through this journey, including rewriting, proofing, and editing can only be by the Grace of God. I am so honored that he and his wife are now a part of my life in such an intimate way and will be into eternity! May the Lord rain blessing on you both and your precious family forevermore! To purchase a copy of John's book, visit Amazon.com.

About the Author

Doreen Stumpf is full of passion for the Lord which overflows to others in her eagerness to help them discover their value, gifts, and identity in Christ. Over eight years ago, Doreen believed she would write a book, but didn't know what the book would be about until she entered the doors of a residential rehab for women and children. It was at this time that the story began to unfold. Having served in Christ centered Recovery since 2006, Doreen found her calling and passion in women's ministry. To begin with, she became involved with a women's ministry as a client who was herself in need of healing due to the severe wounding in her life. *Stripped of Shame* is intended for adults, young and old, and parents. It highlights the often overlooked fact that real relationships with Christ, others, and ourselves are the true road to a full recovery. Without them we may be easily led astray by the sweet smiles, casual conversations, and false pleasures that can all start at the bus stop! Please visit Doreen at www.strippedofshame.com.

Dear Reader,

I hope you enjoyed <u>Stripped of Shame</u>. I am grateful that you chose to read one of my most complex and emotional projects to date. My story has not always been easy to share, but I am thankful for the opportunity to share it with all of you. I truly hope that the story of my transformation has encouraged you, giving you hope knowing that you are not alone and the promise to heal your broken heart is always available. It's never too late!

You are important to me and I would love to hear your feedback. Please feel free to contact me at:

Email: <u>Strippedofshame@gmail.com</u>
Website: <u>www.strippedofshame.com</u>

I would also like to ask each and every one of you to do me a favor. If you have a few extra minutes after reading this work, please leave a review on either Amazon.com and/or Goodreads.com. Your feedback is very important to me!

Again, thank you so much for choosing to read my life's journey. I look forward to continuing this spiritual pilgrimage with you. Please remember that you too have an unforgettable story and that unforgettable story is you!

Always,

Doreen Stumpf

Made in the USA
Columbia, SC
20 June 2020

10902584R00117